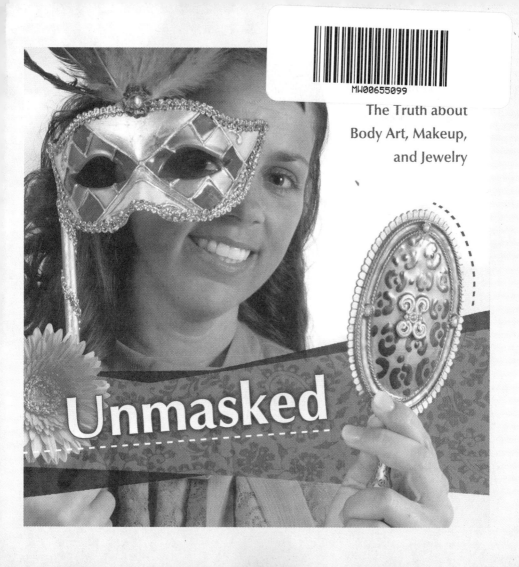

The Truth about
Body Art, Makeup,
and Jewelry

Unmasked

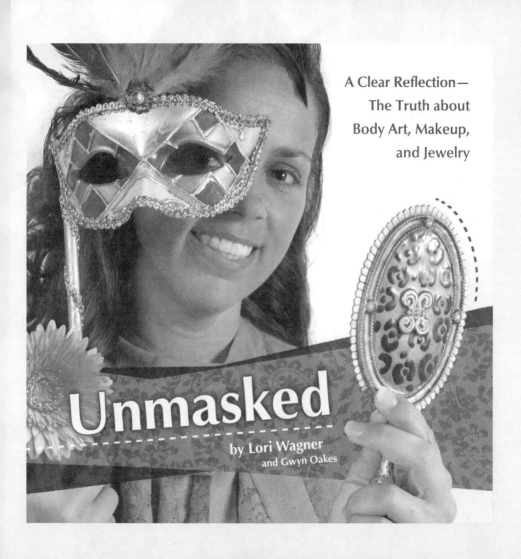

A Clear Reflection—
The Truth about
Body Art, Makeup,
and Jewelry

Unmasked

by Lori Wagner
and Gwyn Oakes

Unmasked
A Clear Reflection—The Truth about Body Art, Makeup, and Jewelry

by Lori Wagner and Gwyn Oakes

© 2012 Ladies Ministries, UPCI

Cover and Interior Design: Laura Merchant

Bible translations used: Unless otherwise noted, the King James Version is the primary Bible translation used. Also included for reference are the New King James Version, New International Version, and Amplified Bible.

Printed in United States of America

A *More to Life* Publication
8855 Dunn Road
Hazelwood, MO 63042

THROUGH GOD'S WORD

Table of Contents

Acknowledgments

Contributors

Vani Marshall
Claudette Walker

Foreword

As a pastor, I am always captivated by the powerful influence of Scripture on sincere believers. Drawing from spiritual insight and volumes of history, the authors of *Unmasked* present a clear path for today's Christian lady. What a powerful treatise for our generation of ladies who desire holiness! This book is vital to the spiritual strength of today's young women—and is the best I've ever read on the topic. The authors have been intentional in providing reliable literature for women of every age, with one purpose in mind: "That the generation to come might know" (Psalm 78:6).

Unmasked is an open door to model biblical truth to spiritually hungry girls and young women. I beg each godly woman to read it and train girls and young ladies to become strong women of faith and virtue. I am convinced this book, along with *The Girl in the Dress* and *Covered by Love,* is more important to the church than ever before.

– Daniel Batchelor
Senior Pastor, First Pentecostal Church, Dupo, Illinois

Introductory Story

"Oh, that poor little girl!" Jackie lifted her fingers to her neck and cupped it protectively in her hand.

"What is it?" Katelyn crossed the bedroom to see the picture in her friend's sociology book. "Aw. Poor baby."

"Can you believe people really do that to themselves? And to helpless little girls?"

"I guess they have to start when they are young," said Katelyn.

"Look." Jackie pointed to the caption under the picture. "It says right here that some begin as early as two years old."

"My niece is two, and she's still wearing diapers," said Katelyn. "I can't imagine putting heavy metal neck rings on a toddler."

"Why do you think they do it?"

Katelyn stared at the picture and shook her head. "I guess they think it's pretty."

"Pretty? Really? It looks painful to me." Jackie flipped to the next page and winced as she focused on its contents. "Look at this woman. She has over a dozen coils around her neck. I don't see how she can move, and her shoulders are messed up."

"You know what my Aunt Evelyn always says: 'It hurts to be beautiful.'"

"Well, that may be, but if it's causing physical pain—I mean, it's deforming these poor women—maybe it's wrong."

"I'm not disagreeing with you, but the fact is, people all over the world hurt themselves to look certain ways they consider beautiful. Look at that guy. What's that called?"

"I call it crazy, but it says here it's 'scarification.'" Jackie turned from the picture that both enthralled and repelled her. "Why would anyone cut patterns in their face like that? I can't imagine how it must have felt."

"We might think it's crazy, but that's what's considered beautiful where he lives." Katelyn turned to the full-length mirror in Jackie's room and swept a wisp of hair back in place. "Every culture has its own definition of beauty, don't you think?"

"I guess so." Jackie sat up on her bed and slapped her textbook closed. "It still disturbs me."

"People every day, right here in our city, get their ears pierced—even little babies who don't have a say. Tattoos are the 'in' accessories these days, and it has to hurt to get those."

"Accessories?" Jackie shook her head in disbelief. "It just doesn't make sense to me why people would hurt themselves to create some kind of 'look.'"

Katelyn walked across the room, swung Jackie's closet door open, and picked up a pair of dress shoes. "OK. I can agree to a point, but the truth is, I know these shoes hurt your feet." Katelyn dangled the towering heels in front of Jackie's face. "You could hardly walk in these at a church service during youth camp, and after it was over, you hobbled across the campground barefoot and in pain."

"I guess that's true." Jackie laughed. "You got me there." She glanced at the book in her hands and then to the Bible on her nightstand. "I don't have a chapter and verse, but it just doesn't seem like it honors God to change what He designed."

"I know," said Katelyn. "But some things are just accepted in culture—even encouraged. A couple of days ago I overheard some girls talking in the locker room after gym class. You know Liz?"

"Yeah." Jackie nodded.

"Well, to be truthful, she did look a wreck. We had just finished a one-mile run and her face was streaked with makeup. She looked like a raccoon from the smudged black eyeliner."

"I can just see her now."

"It wasn't a pretty picture, but I thought what she said was interesting. She refused to leave the locker room until she put her 'face' back on."

"Put her face on?"

"The one she paints on with brushes and sponges and sticks," said Katelyn.

"Hmmm. That's strange—even kind of backwards. We always have our faces on—our real ones, anyway. I think it's sad some people feel they can't go out in public without putting on a false face. It's almost like a mask that hides the person God made."

"Well, like I said, it's part of the way our culture defines beauty. To be honest, a little makeup does seem to enhance a person's features, don't you think—if they don't go overboard, anyway?"

Jackie studied her friend's expression. "I guess it comes down to who defines beauty for you."

"I'm not saying I feel ugly most of the time," said Katelyn, "but there are days, especially when I compare myself to some of the girls at school, I feel kind of plain. Sometimes I think it would be nice to have darker eyelashes or pinker lips—and I think it might help me 'fit in.'"

"I know what you mean, but it goes back to what I was saying before. The Bible says we are fearfully and wonderfully made, and even when I feel different, it just doesn't seem like I should change what God made." Jackie put one hand on her hip and waggled a finger from the other at Katelyn. "And you remember, girlfriend, God don't make no junk."

Katelyn stepped to the window and lifted a suncatcher dangling from the latch. Colorful beams shot across the room. "I know, but I will confess. I haven't really felt like I wanted to wear a lot of makeup, and I'm nowhere near wanting to get a tattoo; but I sure like sparkly things."

Jackie watched the light dance off the suncatcher and sighed. "I know. There does seem to be something in most of us girls that's attracted to glitter. It's a bling thing."

"It's a bling thing." Katelyn giggled. "That sounds like a chapter title in one of those *Pure Path* books."

"You never know," said Jackie. "I heard there was a new one in the works."

"Oh, that would be great. I loved *The Girl in the Dress* and *Covered by Love*. I'd really like to know what the Bible has to say about things like jewelry and makeup and tattoos."

"Me, too," said Jackie. "I feel like in my heart it's not really a big issue, but my head wants to know."

"Well, sometimes my heart and head are both confused," said Katelyn.

"Maybe we don't have the right answers because we haven't looked in the right places."

"Right," Katelyn agreed. "And the right place is probably not the cosmetic counter at the mall."

"Or the latest teen magazine," Jackie added.

Katelyn turned again to the full-length mirror. "I know I'm worth more than my reflection—the outer person—but that's the person everyone sees."

"You're right." Jackie wrapped an arm around Katelyn's shoulder. "And you are beautiful—inside and out."

"Aw. Thanks, Jackie." Katelyn smiled at her friend's reflection. "I guess it all comes back to our priorities and focus again. What are we looking at? The Word or the world?"

"And who are we trying to please? God, ourselves, or others?"

"We must be growing up," said Katelyn.

"Why's that?"

"Because 'words of wisdom' keep popping into my head."

"Like what?"

"I can just hear Pastor saying, 'If we live to please ourselves, we will never be satisfied.'"

Jackie nodded. "My mom and I were talking about a lady the other day, and what she said made a lot of sense."

"What was that?"

Jackie tipped her head and a shy look crossed her face. "Well, I'll be honest. Let's just say this lady Mom was talking about wouldn't make the cover of any magazine—ever. That's why I was surprised when Mom said she was the most beautiful person she knows. I thought about that, and I realized that when I think of her, I think she's beautiful, too. I don't just see the outside but the beauty that comes from the inside. That's true beauty."

Katelyn considered her friend's words before adding her thoughts. "Like the Proverbs 31 woman."

"Right."

"Someone could be drop-dead gorgeous but if they are unkind, it's like Liz's eyeliner running down her face."

"Legit," said Jackie, and both girls laughed.

Jackie made a step toward the door and then turned to Katelyn with an expression of contentment on her face. "I don't have all the answers, but I do have to say I'm glad I don't feel like I have to hide behind a mask. I'm not embarrassed to show the world the face God gave me. I know some people think I'm locked in old-school religious rules, but I don't feel that way at all. I'm free—free to be me—unmasked."

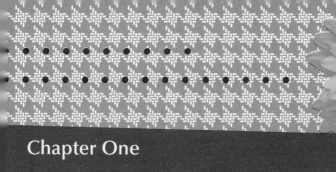

Chapter One

Be-YOU-tiful You!

As you study, please take time to look up and read the verses of Scripture that are noted throughout this book.

Be-YOUtiful You!

Did you know that in America only 2 percent of women consider themselves beautiful?[1] When I first read that statistic, it seemed hard to believe—but then I thought about it. Maybe not.

One look in a world history book should remove any doubt that beauty varies from culture to culture, society to society—even decade to decade within the same culture or society. In one location or period of time, full figures may be all the rage; in another, twiggy figgies are the ideal. One decade's towering curled hairdos will fall to the next's sleek straight designs. Full lips, thin lips. Fair skin, tanned skin. Pointy fingernails, squared tips. Beauty seems to be an ever-changing ideal.

If beauty is a variable or changing quality, who decides what's truly beautiful? Let me give you a simple answer, an answer that will see us all the way through to the end of this book and, hopefully, to any questions you may have.

| **The designer of a "thing" determines when it's complete, when it's worthy, when it's beautiful.** |

Beauty defined is "the quality present in a thing or person that gives intense pleasure or deep satisfaction to the mind."[2] It is an appreciation we receive from: 1) our senses of shapes, color, sounds, patterns, and designs; and 2) personalities which reveal high spiritual qualities.[3]

Beauty is two-fold: Fold One is physical appearance, and Fold Two is the visible aspect of a person's character. See how easy it is to buy into the world's priorities? I should have reversed the order of the folds: Fold One is the visible aspect of a person's character, and Fold Two is physical appearance. We will look at both. As we do, let's keep in mind everything about us should be honoring our Creator, not simply glorifying what He created (Romans 1:25). That includes you and me.

The way we live our lives should point to beautiful Jesus, not whatever beauty He may have bestowed on us. Think about it this way: A sincere walk with God always points to the Cross. The Cross wasn't beautiful, but it did a beautiful work. For us, as it was for Jesus, the Cross is the place where selfishness is crucified for glorious eternal purposes.

> "God is most glorified in us when we are most satisfied in him."
> –John Piper

True beauty can only be defined by God. He alone has the authority to set timeless and unchanging standards. We see snippets of what He considers beautiful throughout His Word. For God, it seems beauty is more a virtue than an appearance (Proverbs 31). That's reassuring to me, because the truth is we are all going to have "bad hair days" and most of us will get old and wrinkly. But that doesn't mean we can't be beautiful. We are more than just "the sum of our parts." True beauty shines from a Christ-like heart.

In this book, we are going to dive into the nitty-gritty details of beauty applications and body modifications. You may have wondered why Christianity has historically shunned tattoos, piercings, and other body modifications, temporary or permanent. We'll look at the historical record, biblical accounts, and hear some personal stories as well.

Please keep in mind this book was written for Christians. It is not meant to finger point at those who are not believers. Its purpose is to bring clarity and instruction for those desiring maturity and purity in their relationships with Jesus.

Much groundwork has already been laid on the principles of love and relationship with God in the first two books of *The Pure Path Series*. I hope you have read *The Girl in the Dress* and *Covered by Love*. They help establish the point that we "do what we do" *because* we love God. Remember, it's simply impossible to earn the right to be in relationship with Jesus. Salvation is a gift—a precious gift that justifies believers.

Paul reminded a group of believers that belonging to God had implications for how they were to live:

| "For ye are bought with a price: therefore glorify God in your body, and in your spirit, which are God's" (I Corinthians 6:20). |

God may not expect unbelievers to follow His principles or walk in His commandments but once we are His, stop the presses! The old story is no more! A new one is now being written; it's a story that's continuing to be written in my life and yours—line upon line, precept upon precept. We don't "live right" to "get" God's promises, but it's *because* of the precious promises of God, who loves us, that we "cleanse ourselves from all filthiness of the flesh and spirit, perfecting holiness in the fear of God" (II Corinthians 7:1). Did you notice that word *perfecting*? It has an "ing" on the end. That means becoming perfect is an ongoing process.

Making Changes

Body modification, also called body alteration, is widely accepted in today's world. I don't know about you, but words like "modification" and "alteration" make me think of clothing being remade. Whatever you call them, these alterations are deliberate changes made to human bodies for non-medical purposes.

Becoming perfect is an ongoing process.

People have bod mods done for different reasons. I've uncovered several, and to be honest, I was surprised by some of them. The point is this: Any body modification is a change to what God designed and created.

My dear friend, I want you to know you are beautiful just the way God made you! Don't let a Photoshopped picture of a model define how you think you should look.

"I praise you because I am fearfully and wonderfully made; your works are wonderful, I know that full well" (Psalm 139:14, NIV). You are God's wonderful work. You've been created in His image, and you

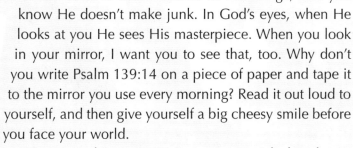

know He doesn't make junk. In God's eyes, when He looks at you He sees His masterpiece. When you look in your mirror, I want you to see that, too. Why don't you write Psalm 139:14 on a piece of paper and tape it to the mirror you use every morning? Read it out loud to yourself, and then give yourself a big cheesy smile before you face your world.

No matter how gorgeous a person might be, there's no escaping the reality that beauty fades over time. That's why it's so important to be more focused on beautiful character than on outer appearance. "Charm is deceptive, and beauty is fleeting; but a woman who fears the LORD is to be praised" (Proverbs 31:30, NIV). There's that deception thing again—hmmm. This verse confirms the higher value of a woman's virtuous character than her physical attractiveness.

BEAUTY 24 FADES.

The New Testament also teaches that beauty should not come from outer adornment (I Peter 3:3-4). Peter instructed believers to reject the customs of Egyptian women who spent hours on their appearance. Instead, he encouraged them to pursue inner, unfading beauty that is more precious in God's sight. That kind of beauty never wrinkles or fades.

True Confession

I go to places all over the globe and see hundreds and thousands of people every year. Many times I have heard speakers say things like, "You are all so beautiful."

Now for the confession. In my heart I would think, "I know there are some ugly ones here. The speaker is just being nice."

Girls, God pricked me in my heart and dropped this on me: "Obedience is beautiful." Those three words changed my perspective. I saw everyone through a new lens. When God looks at His girls living and embracing His ways, accepting who He made them to be, He sees beauty. I do now, too. Thank You, Jesus!

Life is filled with beauty when a beautiful God fills your life.

Living and loving the skin you're in, well, sometimes it can be a challenge. We all have our "less than lovely" days, but how wonderful it is to walk in liberty—free from the expensive and time-consuming beauty regimens that enslave so many. I don't have to put on a fake face to go out in the world. God made my face, and He made yours. He picked your hair color, skin color, and the shape of your lips and hips! **I'm free to be me, and you're free to be you—the wonderful, be-YOU-tiful you God made you to be.** This is a great way to live.

What we see all around us is a call to conform. Celebrities are walking advertisements for every kind of body art. Bonnie Graves, author of *Tattooing and Body Piercing, Perspective on Physical Health*, wrote, "A person's hairstyle, makeup, jewelry and clothing all say something about him or her. The same goes for tattoos and body piercings." That made me wonder what my "look" says to my world.

Rather than displaying our untainted, God-given features, many feel compelled to alter their appearances. The reality is that an "altered appearance" is not reality. It's a mask, of sorts. And why do people wear masks? According to Ted Polhemus, author of *Hot Bodies, Cool Styles: New Techniques in Self-Adornment*, "A mask makes it possible for one person to become another person."[4]

"Masking" occurs at different levels. Some people make drastic statements with all-over body modifications that cry out "I'm not like you." You've seen people like this in the mall with spiked and dyed hair, multiple tattoos and piercings, and dark makeup. Others simply want to "enhance" their appearance in efforts to feel better about themselves—to be more "attractive" or "desirable." Then there are those who want to follow the latest fashion trends. That's understandable. I get that. As Christians, however, **our first priority must be to please God** over self.

What are the two greatest biblical commandments? Matthew 22:37-40 provides the answer:
1) Love God.
2) Love others.

All the laws of God are hinged on these two commandments—all of them! Everything followers of God are asked to do or not do is rooted in loving God and loving others. Changing our appearance, for vanity's sake or to "make a statement," falls in neither of these two categories. It's all about me. It's about what I want and how I feel.

We are Christians everywhere we go! Some people feel comfortable with their appearance at church but the true test comes when they go out in public places. I have concerns when I hear of Christians who dress one way at church and another in public. **A presentation that conforms to the world, not the Word, reveals a person's true allegiance.** I've heard stories of people running into "church kids" in the mall "hiding" who they claim to be. They are Christians camouflaged with the look of the world.

Does that exhibit love for God and others? I'm not a psychologist, but it seems to me this type of behavior is rooted in a need to "fit in" based on fear of being rejected or feeling uncomfortable.

Perfect love casts out fear (I John 4:18). Don't be afraid! The Bible says to let your light shine before men (Matthew 5:16)! Don't camouflage your Christian identity. Let your little light shine! After all, your little light is really His big light carried around inside little you. Does your "cover" match your "story"?

We know God looks at the heart (I Samuel 16:7). It's obvious people look at the outer person. What should they see when they look at believers? Someone who is drawing attention to themselves? Remember Paul instructed the Corinthians to glorify God in their bodies *and* spirits (I Corinthians 6:20). God doesn't want one or the other. He wants both. **We can't glorify God in our spirit and glorify ourselves in our bodies. That's like a duet with one of the singers off-key—and that's not pretty!**

You may never feel drop-dead gorgeous, but by spending regular time with the Lord in prayer and in the Word, you can be some kind of wonderful on the inside. Wonderful on the inside shows up on the outside. Don't forget: Obedience is beautiful!

If you have read *Covered by Love*, I hope you remember that God put all the good stuff, the jewels and precious metals, *inside* the curtains of the Holy Place. His treasures were not on outer display.

More Beautiful You
by Jonny Diaz

Little girl fourteen flipping through a magazine
Says she wants to look that way
But her hair isn't straight, her body isn't fake
And she's always been overweight.

Well, little girl fourteen I wish that you could see
That beauty is within your heart
And you were made with such care, your skin, your body and your hair
Are perfect just the way they are.

There could never be a more beautiful you.
Don't buy the lies, disguises and hoops they make you jump through
You were made to fill a purpose that only you could do
So there could never be a more beautiful you.

(Lyrics copyrighted; permission by Ryan Rettler, *Just-Management.com*)

29

Claudie's Conflict

I remember the day I realized I looked different from the other kids in my public school. I was twelve and a half years old, sitting in class, when my gaze landed on the very modern Billie Headington. Her hair was cut short with bangs. My hair was long and had never been cut. I remember looking at her and then looking at me and thinking, "Man, I look different." Something said, "You're ugly." I thought, "Oh my, oh my, I'm ugly." I went home and looked in the mirror, and from that day, my outlook on life became twisted as I began focusing on "thou shalt nots."

My teacher had given each of the girls in class a little bag of makeup. Mine had a tube of wild rose hot-pink lipstick. I'd never had makeup before. I thought it would be cool to try it so I locked my door and put that hot-pink stuff on my lips. *You're looking fine,* I was thinking. *You're looking a lot better than you do all pale-faced. Everybody at school wears lipstick.* Something began to talk to me about that. It drew me and pulled on me, and it didn't stop at my hot pink lips.

My skirts had always been below my knees. Mama said girls ought to cover their knees, and Mama was always right. I didn't mind—until I was twelve and a half. Everyone else was wearing miniskirts. So when I arrived at school, I went in the bathroom and rolled up my skirt at the waistband. It wasn't really a "mini," but I had a little knee showing so I wouldn't look totally archaic.

This went on for two and a half years. I became more miserable, confused, and upset. I got angrier, more resentful, and became a full-fledged "fence rider." I was in church. I was the preacher's kid sitting on the front row, looking the part on the outside—but in my mind a conflict was raging.

By the time I got to youth camp when I was fourteen, I was a big mess. My motives for going were far from spiritual. I just wanted to be with my friends, and there were some really cute boys coming also.

So I went, and I had a boyfriend there. He bought me hot dogs and hamburgers; it was really cool. On Thursday night, something happened. I don't remember what the preacher said, but I remember all of a sudden I got sick of how I had been feeling. I was miserable at school because I couldn't be like the others; I was miserable at church because I didn't want to be like them. I was miserable everywhere because "a double minded [person] is unstable in all his ways" (James 1:8).

I went to the altar. This was during the old days and the campground tabernacle didn't have even a concrete floor. I walked down the "sawdust trail" and buried my face in wood shavings. I knew it was time to be honest with myself and with God.

I said, "God, I don't even know how to pray, but I'm sick of being a hypocrite. If You would help me, God, and if You could just take this ... this ..." I couldn't even answer because I didn't know what it was. I started crying, and the Holy Ghost said to me "love of the world."

"That's what's wrong with me!" I loved the world. I loved the look of it, the smell of it. "Can You fix me?" I prayed. "Could You take something out of my heart that has made me a miserable wretch for the last two and half years?"

I began to cry and God began working. He was taking away all that twisted confusion. I don't remember anything else. I was lost in the Spirit for hours.

When I got up at midnight, it felt like a thousand-pound load had been lifted off my chest. I knew God had done something, but I also knew that going back to school would be the real test.

I was fine at church. I fit in. When I went back to school in the fall, I was amazed. I no longer envied those girls or wished I could be like them. At the first student council meeting, I listened as they described their summer. I heard about the guys they had slept with and how they had gotten so drunk they puked all over the car and on and on. Tales of their so-called "freedom" caused me to have to excuse myself. I hurried into the bathroom and began to weep. These tears were different from last year's tears of self-pity. I wasn't crying to be like them. I was crying for them, saying, "Oh, God, save my friends. **Thank You for showing me Your beautiful ways. Thank You for saving me from the love of the world**."

I was glad to be different, to look different, act different, and talk different. That was over four decades ago. I can tell you that at one honest prayer meeting, God can change your heart. You don't have to live in confusion. It can be settled. Jesus can change your heart if you want Him to. You can live the rest of your life desiring and loving the things of God and not longing for the things of the world.

Chapter Two

Permanent Bod Mods

The New Ancient Practice of Tattoos, Piercings, and More

Permanent Bod Mods:
The New Ancient Practice of Tattoos, Piercings, and More

Body modifications, making deliberate changes to the human body for non-medical reasons (like plastic surgery, piercings, and tattoos) have become obsessions in North America. We're going to look at some of their historical, scriptural, and practical aspects. A quick list of basic motivators behind body altering includes:

- Artistic appeal
- Rite of passage
- Religious or mystical reason
- Group membership or affiliation
- Loyalty
- Shock value
- Sexual enhancement
- Self expression

Keep in mind this book is written for Christians, so let's make sure we look at bod mods from that perspective. Many people who get tattoos, piercings, and other body adornments and alterations don't understand their origins or associations. A believer's motivations should be different from those of a nonbeliever's.

What's accepted or approved by society has drastically changed over the last few decades. It's no wonder that as our nation slips further from the biblical principles on which it was founded, the face of our culture is changing as well. Sectors of society are looking more primitive, sometimes even barbaric as in the case of the "modern primitives"—people tattooed and pierced so extensively they look like tribal warriors of days gone by. Like the title of this chapter says, it's a new ancient practice, a revival of primitive body alterations. Let's begin with a look at tattoos.

Tattooing

Our western Judeo-Christian culture has not traditionally approved of tattoos. Not everyone who gets tattooed does so with "wrong" intentions. I'm sure many are aware of the rebellious associations or pagan origins of tattoos, but there are those who are clueless. They simply don't believe or understand that what they consider body art is an expression of resistance against the foundational values of their parents, the Christian church, or Judeo-Christian culture. Celebrities and sports figures are wearing tattoos, and that creates a desire in others to get them as well.

The earliest evidence of tattoos comes from Egypt. One of the best-preserved mummies is of Amunet, a priestess worshiped with drunken orgies in temples throughout their land. She was tattooed with lines running up and down her arms and thighs and a symmetrical curved pattern between her naval and privates.

Mike Pearson, a professor of archeology, recorded that many of the dot patterns found on old mummies have been "interpreted as the supernatural force," or spiritual tattoos "taking hold of one's body."[5] We'll see a connection between spirituality and tattooing throughout this chapter.

Mummies with tattoos were also discovered in the Altai Mountains in Central Asia and Western Europe. These "Pazyryk mummies" have many tattoos of animals in which half were mythical, composite beasts.[6] That's scary, if you ask me.

Illustration of a Pazyryk chief from around 500 BC

In the ancient Japanese culture, tattooing was done for cosmetic, decorative, and religious reasons. It was also used to identify and punish criminals. When I read that, it reminded me of the famous novel, *The Scarlet Letter*. In this, a woman who committed adultery was forced to wear a red "A" as punishment for her sin. In a nutshell, the red letter became a symbol of her identity—one that displayed the beliefs of her society.

Ancient Greeks and Romans used tattooing to indicate status or clan membership. Tattoos made it clear to all if a person was enslaved or free. They also tattooed for religious, mystical, and spiritual reasons like ancestor worship, life and death rituals, and "curing procedures."

It's interesting to note that tattooing slaves was outlawed after Christianity became the predominant religion in Europe. Throughout the pages of history, every time Christianity appears, tattoos disappear, with the sad exception of the day in which we are living.

Hindus believe the body is a container. The container eventually dies, but not the energy or the "self" within. Indian Hindus pierce during religious festivals "as a means of enduring pain and suffering, removing bad karma, and ending the cycle of death and rebirth."[7]

The Aztec people were obsessed with piercing and bloodletting. They used both for punishment. They also self-mutilated and sacrificed children, using blood from the rituals to anoint their idols.[8] These aren't pretty pictures, but they do seem to confirm the findings of people who have studied and participated in tattooing.

The Lakota, a Native American tribe primarily from the region of North and South Dakota, continue to practice the ancient Sun Dance, a religious ceremony that can involve piercing both men and women. Some Native American cultures have used branding, skin stripping, and have even removed fingers in honor of their deceased. Many modern-day Native Americans continue to tattoo magical symbols like dream catchers to "catch good spirits and ward off bad."[9]

Between 1914 and 1923, thousands of Armenian women and children were kidnapped. They were integrated in Turkish families, forced to adopt Islam, marry Muslim men, and be marked with specific tattoos. "Tattoos were extensively used as amulets in the Middle East and Islamic countries, with the wearers believing that the mark imbued them with magical powers … and provided protection, strength or fertility. These new markings represented new belonging and marked change in their life."[10] Forced or voluntary, tattoos mark a change—a change in your inner person making a display on the outer.

We are so much more than bodies. We are something special, and something eternal. Remember this as well: If you have been marked by things that happened to you against your will, or against your own good judgment at the time, those marks don't define who you are today. I heard this line in a song recently: "You are more than the sum of your past mistakes." It's true! It's true for you! And me, too, thank God!

Old Testament · · · · · · · · · · · · · · · ·

A key Old Testament verse of Scripture on the subject of tattooing is Leviticus 19:28: "Ye shall not make any cuttings in your flesh for the dead, nor print any marks upon you: I am the LORD."

Since ancient times, people have performed flesh cutting and bloodletting rituals. These practices were believed to release demonic or supernatural powers. In Leviticus 17:11, we read "the life of the flesh is in the blood." This is a likely reason pagans attempt to tap into and unleash this "source of power" through cutting.

I never thought about it before, but I learned that every time a person is tattooed, they bleed. It made me think that when a person tattoos, the images they receive are "baptized" in their own blood. OK. That's kind of creepy.

Facts Are Facts

As you read this chapter, notice most of the quotes come from pro-tattoo or historical sources, not Christian commentaries or Bible studies. Historian Dr. W. D. Hambly stated: "Tattooing originated in connection with ancient rites of scarification and bloodletting which were associated with religious practices intended to put the human soul in harmony with supernatural forces and ensure continuity between this life and the next."[11]

That's a bunch of big words, but what he's saying is tattooing began with ancient pagan religious practices. There's no doubt that cutting and marking skin is rooted in the demonic practice of bloodletting. This also includes scarification, a form of bod mods that permanently changes the skin by making tiny cuts and inserting dyes, sometimes burning and branding the skin.

Leviticus 19:28 underscores the religious or spiritual overtones of this subject. Let's read the verse in context: "Ye shall not make any cuttings in your flesh for the dead, nor print any marks upon you: I am the LORD." The verse concludes with **"I am the LORD."** It's like a big exclamation point that reminds Israel of their covenant relationship with Him.

If a person purposefully sports tats in the house of God, knowing they received them contrary to God's desire and not really caring, how could that possibly be considered "reverencing His sanctuary?" If you are a Spirit-filled believer, you *are* His sanctuary, His tabernacle, His dwelling place.

When we read verse 28 in its setting, we see that tattooing is mentioned right smack dab in the middle of verses about ancient pagan practices. Did God absentmindedly drift "off topic"? I think not. This entire passage is about pagan worship. A *pagan* is one who worships many gods (it also includes those who have no religion) and the *hedonistic,* which means devoted to their own pleasure and self-gratification.

Let's look at what some commentary writers have to say about verse 28.

The New Manners & Customs of the Bible: "Tattooing Forbidden. Both cutting and tattooing were done by the heathens, and so God forbade His people from doing so in imitation of them."[12]

The Book of Leviticus: "The custom of tattooing was forbidden, while among all the nations of antiquity it was common."[13]

Because of their pagan origins, the Lord forbids tattooing in the Old Testament law. I read that orthodox Jews would not allow tattooed people to be buried in their cemeteries. Rabbi Jeffrey Goldwasser commented: "In general, Jewish law does not permit the intentional defacement of the human body. Many Jews are repulsed by the idea of marking their bodies in the way that the Nazis marked the bodies of their victims."[14] Hitler tattooed Jewish captives knowing it was a humiliation and against their religious beliefs.

Rabbi Goldwasser asked: "What would you gain by having a permanent tattoo placed on your body? It will not make you a better person. If you imagine that it would make you feel better about yourself, you may have issues about your self-image that no tattoo will solve."[15] Interesting insight, Rabbi.

History Speaks

Constantine, the first emperor of Rome, prohibited tattooing on the grounds that, "as we are fashioned in God's image, it is sacrilege to modify such a divine creation."[16] Not only would tattooing alter the person God made us to be, it also puts the focus on our fleshly person and can lead to narcissism. That's a big word. Let me give you the definition.

Narcissism:

1. inordinate fascination with oneself; excessive self-love; vanity
2. *Psychoanalysis.* erotic gratification derived from admiration of one's own physical or mental attributes

Being narcissistic means we are immature and self-focused. It reminds me of a quote by Ben Franklin: "People who are wrapped up in themselves make small packages." I want to live my life for something greater than me.

A couple more verses: "And they cried aloud, and cut themselves after their manner with knives and lancets, till the blood gushed out upon them" (I Kings 18:28). This is referring to the Baal worshipers on Mount Carmel during a confrontation with the prophet Elijah. It was their custom to disfigure themselves in worship to their gods.

"Ye are the children of the Lord your God: ye shall not cut yourselves, nor make any baldness between your eyes for the dead" (Deuteronomy 14:1). God does not want His people to follow the practices of the pagan cultures around them.

Many tattoos are sexual in nature and are placed in areas of the body that spark curiosity to see more. They are meant to "enhance" a person's sexuality. This would be a good reason for a single Christian girl to honestly consider her motivation behind getting a tattoo.

Morbid Associations

In a tattoo shop, you will see pictures of skulls, demons, serpents, flames, snakes, grim reapers, spiders and spider webs, and more. Some might say, "It's just artwork," but why would a tattooist display in his shop or on his body demonic pictures of the underworld?

What do these images promote? Life or death? Heaven or Hell? Is it a coincidence that the majority of tattoos would be considered "the dark side" or fantasy? Can we deny the associations?

Some say people wear morbid tattoos as types of amulets or charms to ward off the very evil they represent. Keep in mind these comments are being made by pro-tattoo people, not your Sunday school teacher. It is from their own research that they have arrived at these conclusions, not scriptural study.

New Testament

In Mark 5:2-5 we learn about a man with an unclean spirit. He lived among the tombs of the dead and cut himself. He was known to be demon possessed and his story provides a New Testament association between cutting and bloodletting, demonism and the occult.

We may not find a New Testament verse that expressly forbids tattoos, but there are many verses and principles that apply. "Do you not know that your body is a temple of the Holy Spirit, who is in you, whom you have received from God? You are not your own; you were bought at a price. Therefore honor God with your body" (I Corinthians 6:19-20, NIV).

This verse puts things in perspective. Could a tattoo show honor to God in the physical display of our bodies if He asked us not to get it? Or, for younger readers among us, what if we go against the known desires of our parents? Scripture plainly states, "Children, obey your parents in all things: for this is well pleasing unto the Lord" (Colossians 3:20).

The fact that tattoos are controversial means we should make sure we have solid biblical answers.

The fact that tattoos are controversial means we should make sure we have solid biblical answers on the subject based on the Word—through God's eyes, not our desires. We belong to God, and tattoos are like graffiti on the wall of God's holy temple.

Throughout the New Testament, the Lord has given instructions to His people about their conduct, appearance, and connection to worldly things. He's asked us to:

- Keep unspotted from the world (James 1:27).
- Abstain from even the appearance of evil (I Thessalonians 5:22).
- Don't befriend the world (James 4:4).
- Don't be in agreement with the temple of idols (II Corinthians 6:16).
- Be different, separate from the world and its customs (II Corinthians 6:17).

I realize this is a list of "don'ts." I prefer to focus on happy "dos," but sometimes we have to take an honest look and make sure we're lining up on both the "dos" and the "don'ts."

Our Witness

Regardless of God's express desire, some still believe they are free to do as they wish with their bodies. After studying Scripture and learning the history of tattooing, I hope you have not reached that conclusion. If you have, and you are a professing Christian, I ask you to consider this: If others, in the church and out, would associate me with the ungodly, **what is more important: my witness or my "freedom"?** Would my choice to decorate my body instead of considering my Christian witness be considered preferring one another (Romans 12:10)? Walking worthy of my calling (Ephesians 4:1)? We are called to be ministers of reconciliation (II Corinthians 5:18). Would my tat draw people to God or cause them to question my allegiance to Him?

Some tattoo biblical symbols on their bodies, but **there's no more powerful outward expression of our love for God than walking in obedience to His Word** (I Samuel 15:22).

Most Christians look at someone covered in skulls, swords, and flames and have enough spiritual discernment to know "that's not godly." When it

WHat is MoRe iMPoRtaNt: My WitNeSS oR My "FreedoM"?

comes to someone wanting a "cute" or "harmless" tattoo like a butterfly or even the name of Jesus, it's not as easily grasped. According to the Bible, all tattooing is wrong—not just the grim reaper flash. Regardless of how innocent the picture looks, all tattoos have the same pagan origins.

If you already have a tattoo and are feeling conviction or regret, be assured that God's love covers all our past mistakes and poor decisions. Don't allow anything from your past to keep you from serving God in the now with all your heart, mind, and soul. I want to walk in His blessings, don't you?

Modern Primitives

Most mod privs take pleasure in violating laws or moral codes and going beyond accepted boundaries—in one simple word: sin.

When one with tattoos and piercings sees another with the same, they know, without saying a word, they have something in common. Their attempts at being their own individual self actually conform them into another image, a society that has its own distinguishable social traits.

> **"Tattooings are not only ornaments ...
> they are also messages fraught with spiritual
> and moral significance."**
> – Claude Levi-Strauss, the "father of modern anthropology"
> (the study of humanity)

Piercing

The practice of piercing originated thousands of years ago. Although it is a more accepted practice, the biblical mandates against it are the same ones we studied previously. Remember, "cutting" also means "penetrating." We can't get a piercing without penetrating the skin.

In western society women began piercing their ears in the 1920s. If you will recall from *Covered by Love*, the second book in *The Pure Path Series*, this is the same decade women began cutting their hair, during the rebellious "Roaring Twenties." An ear lobe was where piercing began. In the late 1960s, men began piercing their ears. Homosexual men, in particular, began getting their left ear pierced to communicate their sexual preference. Before long, men were getting both ears pierced, and what began as an effeminate symbol made a surprising turn as "tough guys" began sporting earrings. Soon piercers became more adventurous: noses, eyebrows, lips and tongues, and even private areas of the body.

Founder of the Modern Primitive Movement, Fakir Musafar, believes his body is his to use. He denies the Christian faith claiming "Jehovah was invented."[17] He says about his body, "It's my media, my personal living canvas and living clay to mold and shape and mark as an artful expression of the life energy that flows through it. Your body belongs to you. Play with it."[18]

The living skin of a human being made in God's image hardly seems the right "canvas" for a mere human to mark up with their tools and inks. When asked the question, "How much has body modification got to do with sexuality?" he answered, "A lot!"[19]

> "You put a tattoo on yourself with the knowledge that this body is yours ... and nobody else can control (supposedly) what you do with it. That's why tattooing is such a big thing in prison."
> — Don Ed Hardy, American Tattoo Artist and author of *Tattooing the Invisible Man*

Musafar states, "When you pierce somebody, you're not just piercing a physical body, you are doing some very strange things to the energy circuits and to the spirit that lives in the body."[20] He said people have a "desperate crying need to belong, to find a place and some kind of meaning."[21] It seems to me the desperate crying need is not physical or mental. It is spiritual.

Musafar's approach to spirituality is to use piercings, tattooing, psychedelic drugs, and painful rituals (like hanging from flesh hooks) that take the body first and "drag the feelings and the mind with you."[22] But it's a faulty concept, one that leads him and others to believe that their higher self is "The Great White Spirit," and that spirit is accessible by hanging from flesh hooks. Does that sit in your spirit the way it sits in mine? It makes my stomach turn and my heart hurt—both at the same time.

Ted Polhemus, author of *Hot Bodies, Cool Styles: New Techniques in Self Adornment*, wrote: "The appeal of piercing today may not only be the decorative possibilities it provides but—perhaps even more so—the painful process it requires."[23]

If people feel uncertain about where they fit in, then they may be driven to create their own "places." When I get that "floaty" feeling, like I don't belong, I scramble for something solid, an anchor for my bobbing boat. I'm thankful for the Word of God that lets me know my hope in God is an anchor, sure and steadfast (Hebrews 6:19).

I know we've hopped out on a bunny trail of sorts here, joining piercing and tattooing in the same category—but indeed they are. The pro-tattoo people are not practicing simply because it's artistic or decorative. They are practicing a faulty approach to life and God.

The Spiritual Experience

Tattooing and piercing have often been considered spiritual experiences. John Rush, author of *Spiritual Tattoo*, said he "felt a sense of calm after a tattoo session and somewhat lethargic for the following 12 to 15 hours."[24] He said that after tattooing, he never felt completely undressed. There's something about showing off a tat that pushes against modesty.

The pain of receiving a tattoo is often related to a purging of sorts. "Self-inflicted pain, as in the process of tattooing, causes endorphin dumping, which suppresses chemicals involved in our sensations, while also moderating emotions."[25]

You know about endorphins. They are responsible for that delicious sense of "feel good" after eating chocolate. They are also produced by exercise, excitement, spicy foods, love, sexual activity—and pain. Endorphins work to produce feelings of wellbeing.

> **"I like the way getting a tattoo feels. If I'm depressed, it's nice to get one and deal with the pain. I have one all the way down to my ribs. It hurt, but it felt good— like twisting a loose tooth."[26]**
> – Megan Fox, 2008

I have to follow that quote with an update. At the age of twenty-five, Megan regrets a tat she had done at nineteen. As of this writing, she has been undergoing painful treatments to remove an image on her arm. "Getting them is not that bad," she said, but there is incredible pain to have them removed. "Your skin sort of explodes and looks like little kernels of popcorn popping up."[27]

John Rush says: "For many hours or even days after a session there is a sense of calm and feeling of accomplishment."[28] He adds that the "mingling of pain, pleasure, calmness, or feeling of accomplishment go together to reinforce the event in anticipation of another session. Thus tattooing can be addictive."[29]

According to people who pierce and tattoo, one just doesn't seem to be enough. It gives the impression of opening a door of desire for more. Rush states: "A tattoo is not strictly itself, the ink under the skin. The tattoo (piercing, scar, implant, etc.) is a door."[30] Which leads to the question: a door to what?

Tattoo Today

"Until recently, in the U.S., tattoos often were considered a macho thing," says Bonnie Graves in *Tattooing and Body Piercing, Perspective on Physical Health.* "Many people considered tattoo shops dangerous and socially unacceptable."[31]

WHEN people start doing their "OWN THiNG," SOON aNyTHiNG goes.

Where is the line that marks the difference between cute or cool and abnormal or freakish? If there is a line, who decides where it is drawn? Shouldn't it be God?

My pastor says the greatest form of idolatry in our age is the worship of our own opinion over God's opinion. It's not up to me to determine if I think something's OK or gone too far. The Word of God is the determiner.

Over the ages, women have endured a lot of pain for "beauty's" sake. Rituals for the sake of outward adorning are many and are an attempt to change the bodies God gave us. The Chinese broke the toes, bent them under, and wrapped little girls' feet so tightly they became disfigured and crippled. It was painful, and yet women did this to their daughters because someone decided tiny tootsies were "prettiest." (This practice is now against the law.)

In Africa and Asia, women coil metal rings around their necks, beginning as early as two years old. Padaung women have up to twenty coils that push down their collarbones and necks, and for what reason? Because someone decided an elongated neck was the mark of "ideal beauty." You and I might say these women have taken things too far, but who gets to say how far is too far?

People have pricked, cut, sewn, and hammered their faces to create "decorative" scarring. While turning the pages from one picture to the next of disfigured bodies and faces, the question repeated in my mind: **| When the Word of God is removed from the consideration, where is the line? |**

A non-tattooed body is considered natural, virgin, primitive, or raw. One sales blurb for a company called Modern Primitives stated, "It's not easy making a personal statement or expressing the individual character that defines you in this day and age. Every new form of definition that you find will quickly be copied by society, leaving you to find new ways to express yourself."[32]

It's a never-ending quest.

Life isn't about me making my mark on it. The world was made by God and for His pleasure. Guess what? That includes you and me. Should my aim be to make a "personal statement" or express my "individual character" that "defines me," or should I live a life where people see God's character in me?

The world was made by GOD and for His pleasure.

"Aren't people already unique enough?
Look in the mirror, then look around at others.
Unless you have an identical twin, there is
nobody exactly like you.
When my kids wanted to get tattoos, I told
them to wear the same outfit every day for
a month and then see how they feel about it.
They got the point and are tat free."
– Anonymous, from Brighton, Michigan

A good test when making decisions is to ask yourself, "What's my motivation for doing this?" Everyone is going to mess up along life's way, but I pray our motives, for the most part, are to please the Lord and bring glory to Him—not to please ourselves and bring attention to me, me, me!

In our world, bodies have become mediums for "self-expression." People from all walks of life are sporting piercings and tattoos. We must ask ourselves—I must ask myself—**"What is most important? My look or Who's looking at me?"** Note that capital "w"! The most important "Who" is Jesus!

Aversion to Perversion

Studies have linked tattoos to deviant behaviors such as homosexuality, lesbianism, and sexual perversion.

Ronald Scutt, author of *Art, Sex and Symbol*, writes: "To be fair to those who maintain that tattooing is linked to homosexuality, investigations conducted in a New Zealand Borstal for girls revealed that of the 60 percent tattooed, 90 percent admitted to lesbian behavior."[33] "The most heavily tattooed girls were unstable and insecure and tended to take the masculine role."[34]

A study on tattoos by Dr. Timothy Roberts of Rochester Children's Hospital was published April 2001. Taken from a study of 6,072 young people between the ages of eleven and twenty-one, it is considered one of the most comprehensive investigations of tattoos ever conducted. According to the results, if you have a tattoo, you are:

- nearly four times more likely to engage in sexual intercourse.
- over two times more likely to experience alcohol-related problems.
- nearly two times more likely to use illegal drugs.
- over two times more likely to express violent behavior.
- over two times more likely to drop out of high school.[35]

Dr. Roberts stated: "Tattooing in adolescents was significantly associated with sexual intercourse, substance use, violence and school problems."[36]

Perhaps even more telling, the greater the number of piercings, the greater the abuse of hard drugs such as cocaine, crystal meth, and Ecstasy.[37] More piercings, more drugs. Hmmm.

Remorse and Risks

Part of taking care of our "temples" includes avoiding unnecessary health risks. With every insertion beneath the God-given protective layer of the skin comes risk. Infections, Hepatitis B and C, HIV and AIDS, tetanus, allergic reactions, and nerve damage are all real possibilities. Piercings and tattoos have also been known to cause skin issues that never go away, like sarcoidosis, abnormal scar tissue, allergic dermatitis, photosensitivity, psoriasis, and tumor growth.

The American Red Cross will not allow donors to give blood for twelve full months if they get a tattoo. It's in their guidelines and is related to concerns about hepatitis.

My friend's cousin was paralyzed from the neck down after a reaction to a tattoo. Her organs started shutting down and she almost died. Three years passed. After a long period of time, she is now able to eat solid foods and feed herself, but she still has to wear adult diapers and be dressed and changed by others.

Most people don't know there are real physical risks for those who tattoo. It's not good to be ignorant. In Hosea 4:6, we read, "My people are destroyed for lack of knowledge." It's important to know the risks, physical and spiritual, before engaging in an activity.

In the United States, **most tattooing is done during periods of stress, crisis, or transition.** Author John Rush tells us, "Tattooing, scarification, branding, implants, and self-mutilation are all statements about transitions. Even if a piercing is done for aesthetic/artistic reasons, this is still a statement to the world; you are now different, you have made a transition and 'X' marks the spot."[38]

• •

Conclusion

A tattoo makes a statement that says, "I own my own body," but for a Christian, is that a true declaration? The Bible says we are bought with a price and because of that, we should honor God with our bodies (I Corinthians 6:19-20). Marking our bodies just doesn't seem to line up with Scripture. Piercing and tattooing draw attention to the body. After all, what purpose could they serve but to be seen?

Jesus once said to a woman, "Ye worship ye know not what" (John 4:22), and that can be true when it comes to tattooing and piercings. Please remember, we're not studying this subject to collect an arsenal of information with which to shoot people. We need to be kind and give people the benefit of the doubt. **Sometimes people may worship "they know not what."**

They may even entertain spirits unaware. But guess what? Now *you* know!

The bottom line is this: Consider not only "What would Jesus do?" but "What *did* Jesus do?" Jesus was moved with compassion for the man who cut himself. He delivered him. He didn't join him. Jesus was the spotless Lamb, so it's obvious He didn't have a tattoo. The only marks on His body were those made by the nails that penetrated His hands and feet; the place on His side where He was pierced by a sword; and the whip marks laid upon His back for our healing. These are marks of humility and shame. The marks on Jesus did not glorify His flesh. He received them to save our eternal souls.

Vani's Testimony

In a church service where we were ministering, we preached on how the New Age Movement is infiltrating our churches. One piece of evidence is the rise of body piercings and body modifications that have roots in pagan worship.

James, a first-time visitor to the church, had piercings all over his body. He was a tattoo artist and owner of a tattoo and body piercing shop. At the end of the service, James knelt at the altar. He was seeking the Lord, but something was blocking him.

The Lord showed me that if he would take out the jewelry piercing his body, he would receive the Holy Ghost. I told him, and one by one he pulled them out—from his tongue, belly, chest, nose, and ears. As soon as the last piercing was removed, James received the baptism of the Holy Ghost, weeping and speaking in tongues. He was baptized in Jesus' name that very night. When he rose out of the water, the Lord instantly healed his back of chronic pain.

I learned that James had been raised in church but had walked away from his faith and turned in a dark direction. James went home and told his fiancée about his experience. She came to the next service where God filled her with the Holy Ghost and she was also baptized.

God is able to do all things, and He does all things well. Praise God!

– Vani Marshall

Chapter Three

Bejeweling: It's a Bling Thing!

Bejeweling: It's a Bling Thing!

After our look at body modifications, it should be pretty clear that if flesh must be cut or pierced to wear items of jewelry, this should be the end of the discussion regarding those items.

OK. Now let's look at non-disfiguring jewelry. Part of my research included reading a big fat book called *The Story of Jewelry* by J. Anderson Black. He begins the history of adornment at the dawn of civilization and "proceeds century by century and civilization by civilization to weave the story of the relationship of jewelry to the social, religious, intellectual and economic development of world cultures."[39]

Historically, decorative ornaments were worn in battle to frighten enemies. You might think that's silly, but even today someone might carry a rabbit's foot, St. Christopher medal, or a special stone or crystal they believe has protective powers. These are among many items that would be called amulets or talismans. Throughout history **people have worn these types of small objects because they believed they warded off harm, evil, and illness or brought good luck.** Lucky Charms is more than just a breakfast cereal!

The word *jewelry* comes from the word *jewel*, which evolved in its English form from the old French word *joule*. Beyond that, its roots go back to the Latin word *jocale*, which means "plaything." Interesting!

Jewelry has been used:

- As currency—to display wealth as well as a means of keeping resources safely on a person. Some cultures use jewelry as a method of storing assets. The British Crown Jewels collection, for instance, is the largest in the world and considered priceless.
- For functional purposes—fashioned into clasps, pins, and such. Many items worn for adornment today, like brooches and buckles, began as functional items but over time evolved into decorative pieces.
- As symbols—to show status or membership. Today, among other common symbols, a person might wear a Star of David or crucifix, while someone else might sport a mood ring or peace sign. These adornments reveal affiliations with groups or ways of life. In ancient Rome, for example, only certain social ranks wore rings.
- For personal protection—Amulets, stones, devotional medals, and other items were considered to ward off evil. "In the middle ages, Europeans believed that demons could enter the body through the left ear. Men wore earrings to keep these demons away."[40]
- As an art form—personal decoration and expression.

Let's look at jewelry in specific cultures. Before we begin, I want you to know upfront **the people referenced in *The History of Jewelry* were pagan, or people who did not acknowledge the God of the Bible.**

In Assyria, approximately four thousand years ago, those buried in the Royal Cemetery of Ur, both men and women, wore extensive amounts of jewelry, including amulets, ankle bracelets, and heavy multi-

strand necklaces. It's likely that wearing jewelry was limited to the royals, since I found no mention of common people and jewelry in this era.

In Greece, jewelry was hardly worn and was mostly used for public appearances on special occasions, predominantly worn by women to show wealth, social status, and beauty. It was often supposed to give the wearers protection from the "evil eye" or to endow owners with supernatural powers. Other items contained religious symbolism. Older pieces of Greek jewelry have been found that had been dedicated to their gods.

The most common artifact of Rome was the brooch, which was used to hold clothing together. Ancient Romans also wore signet rings and pendants that could be filled with perfume. Like the Greeks, Roman jewelry was often worn to ward off the "evil eye."

The people of Eastern Europe continued many of the methods of the Romans; however, Christianity became the official state religion. It was a confusing time, a blending of Christianity with the ancient culture of the lands. Religious themes in jewelry were developed in this period, particularly in the wearing of crosses.

The nation of India has a long history of jewelry making. Gold, associated with immortality, was symbolic of the warm sun; silver was symbolic of the cool moon. These were the classic metals used in Indian jewelry and were considered sacred. The people of the Indus Valley Civilization (present-day Pakistan and northwest India) are known for making beads that relate to Hinduism.

The Aztecs used jewelry in sacrifices offered to appease their gods. Their priests killed animal and human sacrifices with gem-encrusted daggers.

Jewish motifs, such as the Star of David and the Hamsa hand, are ancient symbols used in modern Jewish jewelry. They are believed to ward off the negative influences of the "evil eye."

I hope you noticed in these notes from a big, fat history book, there was not one reference made to Hebrew jewelry. Remember, the purpose of *A Story of Jewelry* was to go "century by century and civilization by civilization to weave the story of the relationship of jewelry to the social, religious, intellectual and economic development of world cultures."[41] **There was no record or mention in this book of God's people creating or wearing adornment.**

We find the mention and use of jewelry strictly as ornamentation and appears to have originated in cultures outside the religion of the Jews. It's interesting that in ancient cultures, **many times the same craftsmen who created jewelry also made idols** they decorated with jewels and precious metals. As we continue, you will see a clear biblical link between idolatry and jewelry.

From History Books to the Holy Book

In a seeming contradiction to my last statement, Aaron, Israel's high priest, did wear elaborate ceremonial robes also called

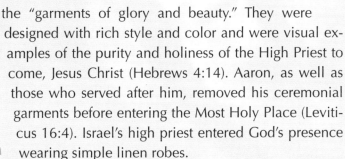

the "garments of glory and beauty." They were designed with rich style and color and were visual examples of the purity and holiness of the High Priest to come, Jesus Christ (Hebrews 4:14). Aaron, as well as those who served after him, removed his ceremonial garments before entering the Most Holy Place (Leviticus 16:4). Israel's high priest entered God's presence wearing simple linen robes.

When Israel wanted to be like the heathen nations around her and demanded a king, Saul was crowned king with a diadem. This was a special cloth headband that had gold and possibly jewels on it. Its purpose, for both the high priest and the king, was to identify the wearer as separated from the people at large. Unlike the crowns of pagans that indicated a person's own power and royalty, these diadems were symbols of holiness to God and that the priest or king was separated and anointed for God's service.

I mentioned this about crowns and diadems because I want you to understand their purpose. They weren't worn just to make folks look dazzling and prettified. God designed the diadem worn exclusively by His one high priest. When He allowed a king to be chosen, outside His original intention for His people, Saul was also given the same sort of headdress. Both of these represented consecration. *Consecration* is a big word, but it basically means dedication to the service and worship of God.

The same Hebrew word for diadem, *nezer,* according to *Gesenius's Lexicon,* also refers to "consecration of a priest," a "consecrated head," like that of a man who has taken a Nazarite vow, and even "the long unshorn hair of a woman."[42] Each of these are symbols of consecration, being set apart for God.

Wow. I never imagined going off on a tangent like this, but did you get that? In *Covered by Love* we discussed how a woman's uncut hair is her glory

(I Corinthians 11:15). Now we're discovering deeper insights. **Uncut hair has the same effect of separating a woman and calling her God's chosen as the diadem worn by the high priest and the first king of Israel.** Incredible!

The Bible tells of different crowns of glory (Proverbs 4:9; Proverbs 16:31; Isaiah 62:3), but none of them refer to ornamental headgear made with precious metals or decorated with stones or jewels. They refer to wisdom, gray hair, and even God's people.

The Bible also references a "crown of pride." "Woe to the crown of pride, to the drunkards of Ephraim, whose glorious beauty is a fading flower" (Isaiah 28:1). This crown will be "trodden under feet" (verse 3). That means it will be stomped on. Its glorious beauty will be like a fading flower (verse 4), but here's the good news from verse 5: "In that day shall the Lord of hosts be for a crown of glory, and for a diadem of beauty, unto the residue of his people." In other words, **there will be a day when earthly crowns are worth nothing, but the Lord will be a crown of glory.**

As a child of God, the adornment to pursue is not a temporary crown with no eternal value, but the "crown of righteousness, which the Lord, the righteous judge, shall give me at that day" (II Timothy 4:8). The "crown of life" is promised to those who endure temptation and love God (James 1:12). And one more verse: "When the chief Shepherd shall appear, ye shall receive a crown of glory that fadeth not away" (I Peter 5:4). That's some good stuff there.

CROWN O

We know the New Testament calls God's people both kings and priests. These titles have spiritual meaning. You and I don't have our own little countries to rule over or marble temples where we serve as priests. The "lands" we rule over don't authorize us to wear real crowns and royal robes. Can you just see yourself strolling through Walmart decked out like that?

| While we are still in this world, our ornamentation should be grace, humility, and smelling good. |

That's not a popular message, but it is biblical: "For all that is in the world, the lust of the flesh, and the lust of the eyes, and the pride of life, is not of the Father, but is of the world" (I John 2:16). From which world do we seek our treasure? This world, or the next? I'm going after the eternal!

"If your right eye causes you to sin, gouge it out and throw it away. It is better for you to lose one part of your body than for your whole body to be thrown into hell" (Matthew 5:29, NIV). Do you think it is a coincidence the Lord used an eye for His illustration in this verse? We see with our eyes. Our focus feeds desire, and desire conceived can lead us down wrong paths (James 1:15). I'm not saying a person is going to Hell because they like to look at sparkly things. That would be silly, but let's be real. If glittery fascinations

GLORY

distract our focus from the eternal, we must use wisdom when it comes to filling our senses with them.

While we're on the subject of being careful (as in "full of care," not care-*less*), we also need to be aware of the effect relationships have in our lives. We become like the people we hang with. Don't underestimate the power of peer pressure. It influences for both good and bad!

Let's look at it from another angle. As is often the case in the Bible, a physical illustration gives a spiritual picture. In Heaven we will wear the beautiful garments of salvation and robes of righteousness. These aren't physical, but spiritual, and they need no adornment. They are perfect as God made them.

| **We are the jewels of God.
We don't wear them—we *are* them.** |

Promotion Time!

Most people want to wear things that make them look and feel good. In a sense, this reveals a sort of self-promotion. God has something to say about promotion: "Wisdom is the principal thing; therefore get wisdom: and with all thy getting get understanding. Exalt her [wisdom], and she shall promote thee: she shall bring thee to honour, when thou dost embrace her. She shall give to thine head an ornament of grace: a crown of glory shall she deliver to thee" (Proverbs 4:7-9).

What really promotes and brings honor to a person is not lifting up "self" but exalting, or lifting up, wisdom and understanding. When we do that, the results are far greater than putting crowns on our own heads. God gives us ornaments of grace and crowns of glory. We become God's ornaments.

Here's another verse: "My son, let them not escape from your sight, but keep sound and godly Wisdom and discretion, and they will be life to your inner self, and a gracious ornament to your neck" (Proverbs 3:21-22, AMP). Inner beauty shows up on the outside. **God wants His people to be jeweled on the inside with ornaments of His grace.** When we carry these on the inside, they will be evident on the outside and touch the lives of others.

Do you want to be "God's jewel"? It's not hard! Those who were called God's jewels in Malachi 3:16-17 were those who reverenced and worshipfully feared the Lord. We can do that, girls! When we fear the Lord and think on His name, we will become His jewels. No wonder Satan wants to do anything He can to keep us from this destiny. We're taking over the job he lost through his rebellion. He once reflected God's glory, but now that honor is given to those who submit to God's will. **Satan is displaced, and rebellion is replaced by submission with reverence and joy—and the results are glorious!**

Jewelry and Idolatry

Let's dive further in to some specifics. When Jacob went to Bethel to build an altar, he told his household, "Put away the strange gods that are among you, and be clean, and change your garments ... and they gave unto Jacob all the strange gods which were in their hand, and all their earrings which were in their ears"(Genesis 35:2-4). Do you find it interesting that the strange gods and earrings were turned over at the same time and for the same reason?

Jacob was preparing to enter into worship at a sacred place. The earrings his family had were obtained in Canaan, an idolatrous nation, and were connected somehow with idolatry. Through Jacob's example, we see that **as people prepared to repent and make atonement before the Lord, they gave up both their idols and their ornaments.** Jacob was willing to lay aside some things in order to obtain God's blessing for himself and his family.

We get another picture of this in Exodus 12:35. When the Israelites were preparing to leave captivity, Egyptians gave gold and silver ornaments. There was a reason this happened. It was not for the Hebrews to wear the jewelry associated with Egyptian idol worship. I believe God was pooling together resources to build His Tabernacle.

Did you know there was a time God was so disgusted with the Israelites He was ready to separate Himself from them? It's true. They were on a collision course with God's boot. He said they were "stiffnecked" and was ready to send them off to the Promised Land—not to bless them, oh no, only to fulfill His obligation to their ancestors. The kicker? The Lord was not planning to go with them. When the people learned of it, they were distressed and began to mourn. Do you know what God said? I found this so interesting. God told them to take off the ornaments they were wearing "that [He] may know what to do unto thee" (Exodus 33:5-6).

Doing so was a sign of humility, and God's response to Moses in verse 14 was that He would go with them and lead them to their journey's end.

> ## We live each moment before the Lord.
> ## Are we walking humbly before Him in our land?

There's no doubt, given these examples, taking off ornamentation humbled the people before God. The Lord does factor in ornamentation in our approach to Him and life. God was ready to wipe the Israelites out in the desert before they ever entered the Promised Land. Before they could go in, they had to take off their ornaments.

Yeah, I know. That's Old Testament. True. But we still use the examples given to us in the Old Testament to define things we do today. Don't just take my word for it. The apostle Paul told us the things written in the Old Testament happened to them as examples and were written as warnings for us (I Corinthians 10:11).

The Old and New Testaments go together like peanut butter and jelly. Just one won't do. We need them both for the complete "sandwich." Can you imagine trying to separate peanut butter and jelly once its maker smashed those slices together? There would be jelly on the peanut butter and peanut butter on the jelly!

I came across a sad story in Judges 8. We've probably all heard the account of Gideon's army and their great defeat over the enemy, but after the battle was won, Gideon flat out messed up. It's ironic, when we look at the details. In verse 23 Gideon refused to rule over the people. He said no, that God would be their ruler. It was a noble declaration, but then what did he do? He asked them for their earrings.

The Bible tells us the men in this land had earrings because they were Ishmaelites (see verse 24). Israelites did not wear earrings. In appreciation for being liberated from the Midianites, the men willingly gave their earrings to Gideon. Now the sad part. Gideon made an ephod out of those earrings. An ephod was one of the high priest's special ceremonial garments. Gideon had no authority to do that, but he did, and he set it up in his home town. The Bible says Gideon and all Israel "prostituted" themselves and were unfaithful to God by worshiping at the ephod made from Ishmaelite earrings (verse 27, NIV).

Oh, Gideon! What happened to the people as a result of your desire for an idol of gold? It reminds me of the calf made by Aaron (Ecclesiastes 1:9).

It's a Bling Thing

It was a backslidden Israel that decked herself with jewelry as in Isaiah 3:16-26. There's a long list given about her ornaments that includes chains, earrings, rings, and nose rings. These individuals, these "daughters of Zion" wearing all the blitz and bling, were referred to just a few verses later as filthy, proud, vain, and haughty (Isaiah 4:4, AMP).

Did the ornamentation make them filthy, proud, vain, and haughty, or did it simply reveal on the outside the truth of what was in their hearts? The end of the verse is a bit scary. The Lord declared He would wash away their moral filth by "the spirit and blast of judgment and by the spirit and blast of burning and sifting." Cleansing would be brought by judgment and burning. That does not sound like a walk in the park to me. We see the people who were to be cleansed were destined to be "beautiful and glorious" (Isaiah 4:2). God cleansed. God beautified. God glorified—and without worldly ornamentation.

Compare these immoral daughters of Zion to the pure bride of Christ mentioned in Revelation 19:7-8. This woman made herself ready. She wore "fine linen, clean and white." There's no mention of this Bride wearing anything to call attention to herself—no makeup, no bracelets, no pearls. She is the pearl. She is the treasure, polished and readied (Psalm 144:12). She is called "comely and delicate" (Jeremiah 6:2). That means she is beautiful, not brash, boastful, or loud.

That reminds me of the words in the famous "love chapter": "Love is patient, love is kind. It does not envy, it does not boast, it is not proud. It is not rude, it is not self-seeking, it is not easily angered, it keeps no record of wrongs. Love does not delight in evil but rejoices with the truth" (I Corinthians 13:4-6, NIV).

We find another link between jewelry and idolatry, unfaithfulness, and ornamentation in Hosea: "I will visit upon her the days of Baalim, wherein she burned incense to them, and she decked herself with her earrings and her jewels, and she went after her lovers, and forgat me, saith the LORD" (Hosea 2:13). God wasn't talking about a social visit, but punishment.

It's hard to deny the association between worshiping false gods, wearing ornamentation, and unfaithfulness. Wearing ornaments seems to be a visible symbol that the Lord's beloved had departed from doing His will. It reminds me of the sinful woman that represents the false church. We read about her in the last book of the Bible: "The woman was dressed in purple and scarlet, and was glittering with gold, precious stones and pearls. She held a golden cup in her hand, filled with abominable things and the filth of her adulteries" (Revelation 17:4, NIV). Do you see the connection of false religion, ornamentation, and unfaithfulness?

Baubles, Frippery, and Stuff

We looked at hair and hairstyles in *Covered by Love*. I would like to put in a reminder that our everyday hairdos should not be overly elaborate or intertwined with "hair jewelry" and bling. If we're walking through the mall with a hairdo that looks like a Christmas tree, well, that's not moderate or modest. It's peculiar, but that's not the kind of peculiar Scripture calls God's people to be (I Peter 2:9). Folks shouldn't be able to pick up Wi-Fi on some girl's outrageous hair bling.

One thing some forget when it comes to modesty is stewardship—stewardship of our bodies as well as our resources. Spending money on extravagant clothes and jewelry for the sole purpose of satisfying our sensual desires might well fall into the category of poor stewardship.

The type of embellishment that won't bite into your missions giving, the kind that gets the right kind of attention (God's), is a meek and quiet spirit (I Peter 3:4). God is attracted to that kind of ornamentation. He likes it when we wear humility, godliness, and good works with modesty and moderation. And think about this: If we are to be like Jesus, have you ever read in the Bible of Him wearing jewelry?

But What About ...

What about other people mentioned in the Bible who wore jewelry? In Genesis 24:47-48, we read that Rebekah was given jewelry as an engagement gift. You might have wondered what that was all about.

Here's the scoop. Abraham was looking for a bride for his son Isaac in a land of pagan people. These were his relatives, but they were not God worshipers. Previously God had instructed Abraham to leave his country and family (Genesis 12:1). He was obedient to the Lord, but when it was time to get a bride for his son, he sent his servant back to find one from among his relatives who still lived in Mesopotamia. It was appropriate to offer the customary bridal gift in the culture from which the wife was coming. It would have been an insult to do otherwise.

That's like saying, "I know it's your long heritage to get 'X' for a bride, but how about I give you 'Y' instead?" It just wasn't done.

In Genesis 41:42, the Egyptian Pharaoh gave Joseph a ring, clothes, and a gold chain. Remember that Joseph wasn't in Egypt on vacation. He had been forced into slavery in a pagan nation for many years. Several of those years were spent in prison. Joseph did not have the option to wear the clothing of his people. With the ring, clothes, and chain, the Pharaoh was giving Joseph more than adornments: they were symbols of power. The signet ring from his own hand was a sign to all the people that Joseph was acting on Pharaoh's behalf. This example goes back to the crowns we discussed earlier. Joseph did not choose to wear these items to adorn himself but was given them to identify his new office among the Egyptians.

What about in the New Testament? In the story of the prodigal son, the father put a ring on his son's finger (Luke 15:22). Yes, he did. The ring on the hand was the father's way of restoring dignity and allegiance to his son when he returned home in rags from his party gone bad. According to *Barnes' Notes on the Bible*, only wealthy families and those in office commonly wore rings.[43] They identified their offices or family membership. I could say my name is Hilton or Rockefeller, but that's not going to get me anywhere without proof. It's easy to see why having one of these official rings would be desirable among the common people during the time Jesus told the prodigal's story. They were symbols of a person's elevated status and authority.

We talked about the list of ornaments the Lord gave Israel in Ezekiel 16. This portion of Scripture is speaking figuratively about the nation as a whole. The Lord was referring to how He had lifted the nation out of their filth and shame and raised them to a place of honor.

God said Israel's beauty was perfect through His "comeliness," meaning His majesty and splendor, which He had put upon her (Ezekiel 16:14).

What made Israel beautiful? It wasn't literal crowns and jewels and expensive clothes. God put His honor and glory upon her. And what did she do with the treasure He gave? Nothing good! Read the rest of the chapter; it's a disheartening story of unfaithfulness, idolatry, and even child sacrifice.

Oh, that we would treasure the gifts of God's honor, majesty, and splendor. He has given us His glorious Spirit! How will we respond to His goodness? I want to do better. Not just better than the people written about in this chapter in Ezekiel, but better than I've been doing so far. Let's press on toward the mark for the high calling (Philippians 3:14)! That's talking about excellence! Let's walk worthy of God who called us into His kingdom and glory (I Thessalonians 2:12).

Here's another Old Testament example. There are two ways to look at the bounty the Israelite's took from Egypt. I believe God told them to ask for the jewelry of the Egyptians to provide for His Tabernacle. But let's look at it from another perspective. Suppose God just wanted them to have those pretty things for themselves as a reward for all their years of labor? On the narrow chance that was true, let's look at their reaction. What did the people do with their Egyptian bounty? They took those earrings and made a golden idol out of them (Exodus 32:1-7). They turned their back on the God who delivered them and blessed them.

When the Lord corrected Israel for being haughty, with outstretched necks, flirty eyes, and tinkling jewelry, He gave a list of all the things the women counted on for "bravery": their jewels and fine clothes (Isaiah 3:18).

Their fancy apparel and adornments caused feelings of glory and splendor. In the *King James Bible*, **one of the items listed in this passage as "earrings" is translated from a Hebrew word *lachash* specifically associated with witchcraft.**

Lachash literally means:
a) serpent-charming,
b) charms, amulets (worn by women)

Since the list in Isaiah referred exclusively to physical things being worn, it seems logical that in this case earrings were actual charms or amulets.

Old Testament or New, God doesn't just wink at witchcraft. In I Samuel 15:23 it's clearly identified as sin. Those who practice witchcraft are in the list of them that "shall not inherit the kingdom of God" (Galatians 5:21).

I'm not saying people today wear earrings with the intent to cast spells. I am simply giving the account of the original root word used in Scripture. Over and over we see in biblical times that wearing earrings was connected with idolatry and/or haughtiness. Could people unknowingly open doors to pagan influence in their lives through piercing and ornamentation?

Dressing vs. Decorating

Ladies, we have to wear clothes. This is where moderation comes in. We need to wear shoes. Almost every girl carries a bag of some sort to hold her ID, keys, etc. It's OK to pick cute stuff. I (in agreement with the publishers of this book) am not saying you should make a drab presentation of yourself to the world for modesty's sake. **The key is keeping things in balance and perspective—not going overboard one way or the other, using a biblical basis for your choices.**

balance & perspective

Decorative ornamentation is more than jewelry people wear. It can also include things carried like phones, pens, purses, glasses, etc. You may even have seen a picture of a starlet accessorizing with a designer pooch in her pocketbook or on her arm! Yes, it's possible that a living, breathing animal could be used as an ornament. Accessories, and even people, have been called "eye candy," items that are attractive to look at but don't contribute anything essential.

With exceptions, such as medical alert bracelets or military dog tags, jewelry normally differs from other items of personal adornment in that it has no other purpose than to look appealing or send a message.

Let's move to a topic that has some room for discussion and personal opinion: accessories that are useful but are also considered ornamental. Remember our discussion of standards in *The Girl in the Dress* and how they basically fall into three categories: biblical, church standards, and personal convictions. There are some things your pastor or parents might have personal convictions about. I strongly advise you to follow the guidance of your spiritual leaders when it comes to what you choose to wear.

Rings

There are several schools of thought in the Christian community on the subject of wearing rings. Some do not see any question that rings are in "the list" in Isaiah 3 so they don't wear them—period. I understand and respect their sincere desire to please the Lord.

Should a Christian wear a wedding ring? As I see it, there may be three answers:

No way!

Absolutely!

Maybe ... ?

We already discussed the "no way" perspective, and I again affirm that choice if that is someone's personal conviction. Those who say "absolutely" usually consider a wedding ring a public symbol of "non-availability," a safeguard for their marriage. When I was single, I admit to looking at men's hands to see if they wore a wedding ring. If they did, well, my potential-husband radar detector dropped from "alert" to "standby."

For those who fall in Category 3, who see both sides of the issue, I advise that you follow the guidance of your pastor. If you do wear a wedding ring, please remember moderation. I hope and pray nothing I choose to do or wear creates a stumbling block for others—both in church and those who are not. I want to have a positive impact for the kingdom of God. I want to make sure my use of any "approved" adornments doesn't create confusion by being flashy or showy.

A veteran missionary told of the conviction of the people where they ministered concerning a wedding band. She and her husband had never worn rings but the country in which they were ministering believed strongly in wearing a wedding band as a symbol of marriage. They discussed it, prayed about it, and purchased simple wedding bands. The congregation rejoiced that the missionaries had finally decided to be married and celebrated that fact.

Watches

Watches are also in the category of useful jewelry worn on the body. A watch serves a purpose. For some, a timepiece keeps them on track with their schedules. For others, it lets them know how late they are running (smile). I choose to wear a watch mostly when I am away from home to keep me on schedule. I have seen people wearing watches with flashy bracelets in every color and hue, sparkles and spangles galore. Remember, if you feel free to wear a watch, it should not be for drawing attention to you but serving a function.

Hair Accessories

Hair clasps—get this—were designed to clasp hair. Along with picks, combs, and pins, the hair clasps I choose to wear have function. I'm thankful for hair fasteners. They keep my hair out of my face when I'm cleaning and out of the dirt when I'm gardening. Of course I use them other times as well but the point is, they have a job to do. The level of ornamentation a person

feels comfortable with on their hair fasteners is an individual matter. If we're sticking fancies and sparklies that aren't serving any purpose in our bouffants, it would be worthwhile to consider our motives and stewardship.

Purses

It's fun to get a new purse. I know when I buy a new one that I'm going to keep it for years, so it's worth it to me to get something that will last. I enjoy a bag with some style too.

It's just as easy to get extravagant on purses as with other functional accessories. I have to reign myself in sometimes and ask myself, "Why do I want that one?" Is it because it's got a designer label on it so people will look at it and think, "Oh, she's got *that* brand" or because my purse can wear all the stuff I can't: sparkles, bangles, and baubles? Oh, did I really say that? Um, yes, I did. Moderation, girls.

OK. Let's bring it home now. **An ornament is like an "adjective" that tells something about the "noun" wearing it.** Personal embellishments reveal things about the wearer's attitudes and values. Jewels are symbols of status and wealth. As a Christian, my status is "saved" and my wealth is spiritual treasure that robbers cannot steal and moth cannot corrupt!

As Christians, our status is not evidenced by what we put on our fingers or around our necks. Our "place in this world" isn't in this world at all, and it's the Cross that declares our true station in life. It says you and I are worth more than sparkling stones and shiny metals. We are worth the precious blood of Jesus (I Peter 1:18-19).

Jesus purchased our lives. It's because of His sacrifice we are not our own and are called to "cleanse ourselves from everything that contaminates and defiles body and spirit" (II Corinthians 7:1, AMP). We are called to keep our natural and spiritual lives consecrated in the fear of the Lord. Yes, there are many ways we can defile our "temples." We can abuse medicines and drugs—even food. These practices are to be avoided, as well. They just aren't being covered in this book!

It's been said that the greatest journey is the distance between the heart and the head. Sometimes our heads "get" things our hearts want to disagree with. And sometimes our hearts feel things against which our minds or carnal natures rebel. When it comes right down to it, Romans 8:6-10 makes it clear that our senses and reasoning without the Spirit of God are death; but the mind of the Spirit is life and peace for the soul, for now and forever. Our human minds are hostile to God's Word. That's why when we live to please our flesh, catering to our own carnal natures and appetites, we can't please God or be considered acceptable to Him (see verse 8). But there's good news. When we live for God, He directs our paths; and when we are led by the Spirit, we are the sons and daughters of God (see verse 10).

> ## "The best way to get the Word from your head to your heart is on your knees."
> — Eli Hernandez

There are two types of crowns available to us today. We can seek to crown ourselves on this earth with the world's glory, or we can wear a true victor's crown of righteousness—forever and ever and ever amen! (See II Timothy 4:8.)

If our desire is for the razzle dazzle in this world, we will never be satisfied. Read it yourself in Proverbs 27:20: "The eyes of man are never satisfied." If we open ourselves to things of this world, our roving eyes will create a hunger that won't be filled. What we have will never be enough. As we look at the ads, the windows in the mall, what the stars are wearing—we will always want more.

Many people are willing to talk about the Lord's love and mercy; but when it's time to discuss a lifestyle that requires change or sacrifice, that's altogether different. That takes us to the root of all sin: pride.

What sin isn't rooted in pride? Pride is at the core of every decision we make to choose our way over God's. It began with Lucifer's fall from Heaven, and he carried it into the Garden of Eden, developing in Eve a desire she may never have succumbed to without his questions and his accusations against God.

The Lord offers us more than we could ever give to Him in return. He gives us His Word that our "joy might be full" (John 15:11). Living for the Lord is the most exciting and rewarding life. It comes with challenges, but it also comes with

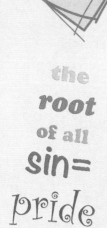

the **root** of all sin= pride

a more rewarding purpose than living for ourselves could ever offer. We can live our days filled with passion and purpose, "perfecting holiness in the fear of the Lord" (II Corinthians 7:1).

Perfecting holiness is about my character being transformed into godly character—thinking like He thinks, loving what He loves, hating what He hates, and acting like Jesus would.

> **Holiness, without a doubt, is:**
> 1) **separation from sin and the world's system, and**
> 2) **dedication to God (Romans 12:1-2; II Corinthians 6:17-7:1).**

What are the three major areas of sin God wants us to avoid? Lust of the flesh, lust of the eyes, and the pride of life. Doesn't outward adorning involve all three of these? My flesh wants to be "prettier"—to enhance certain features and make them appear "better." My eyes say "ooh, sparkly, pretty! Gimme, gimme!" And the pride of life says, "I want that. I deserve that. Why would God withhold that from me? I'm gonna take what I want." Isn't that how Lucifer was thinking before his attempt to make himself equal with God? Isn't this the same approach Satan used when he tempted Eve in the Garden?

Why do you think Satan attacked Eve? Maybe because she was just like me, or maybe like you? Perhaps when she listened to her tempter, it created a lack of security in her or for her future.

Throughout the pages of history, going against God's divine order has resulted in a loss of glory and breakdown of relationships. Satan was whispering then, and he's whispering now: "Did God really say … ?" "Does God really care about … ?"

What was Satan wearing in Heaven? Ezekiel 28:13 tells us he was covered in gemstones. The bejeweled Lucifer was the one who became lifted up in pride—not Michael, not Gabriel.

The Bible clearly teaches that God's people are called to be unspotted from the world (James 1:27). We are not to be friends of the world (James 4:4) or to love the world and the things that are in it (I John 2:15). The apostle Peter gave the following instructions to believers. Keep in mind these were written to Christian women with non-believing husbands, but these verses give real insight as to how we should conduct ourselves in ways that affect the people around us.

"Wives, in the same way be submissive to your husbands so that, if any of them do not believe the word, they may be won over without words by the behavior of their wives, when they see the purity and reverence of your lives. Your beauty should not come from outward adornment, such as braided hair and the wearing of gold jewelry and fine clothes. Instead, it should be that of your inner self, the unfading beauty of a gentle and quiet spirit, which is of great worth in God's sight" (I Peter 3:1-4, NIV).

When the world sees purity and reverence in our lives that comes from inner character and virtue, we have a powerful testimony. We could actually win others to the Lord without ever reciting Romans 3:23, Acts 2:38, or John 3:16. It's been said that one of our most powerful Christian witnesses is a radiant countenance. If we will "unmask" ourselves before the Lord and live continually in His presence, His glory will show up. We receive God's glory, and we reveal that to the world in our expressions and behavior.

I know I've used this word many times in this chapter, but we need to remember to be moderate. Sadly, some "holiness" folks don't get this. I come in contact with a lot of believers from a lot of denominations, and sometimes "holiness" people who follow accepted "guidelines" are much more pretentious in their appearance. Oh, they don't "break the rules," but they do take them to extremes. Remember, the Bible says "let your moderation be known unto all men" (Philippians 4:5). I'm sure that includes women, too! Why? The end of the verse tells us: "The Lord is at hand." Jesus is always near!

Look at the first part of that verse in the *Amplified Bible*: "Let all men know and perceive and recognize your unselfishness (your considerateness, your forbearing spirit)." **That's what the world is supposed to see in you and me.** Ornamental jewelry shouts "look at me!" And when it comes to costume jewelry—like cubic zirconia that costs a fraction of a diamond, looks like one, but isn't—it's flashy and deceptive. What's the point in wearing fake stuff? It's rather like that mask concept again, masquerading by wearing a false appearance of wealth.

If there was ever a "person" who had a right to make a public show of His impressiveness, it was the Lord Jesus Christ. Jesus chose a humble path. He rode into Jerusalem on a donkey, a symbol of His humility (Zechariah 9:9; Matthew 21:5). His crown held no jewels, but thorns.

Chapter Four

Put On a Happy Face

Put On a Happy Face

It's time to talk about makeup. First, let's be clear on this point: **There is a big difference between hygiene products and appearance altering, colorful cosmetics.** If you have dry skin, by all means slather on a moisturizing lotion. When your pucker gets parched, glide on a soothing lip balm. Everyone uses products of some sort to cleanse hair and bodies. Good grooming is important. Take care of the masterpiece God made. That would be you.

As we've already discussed, many people are less than satisfied with their God-given features. They look for ways to make them feel better about their appearance or perhaps what they think will cause them to be accepted by others. **|True beauty is not something we can paint on or put on.|** True beauty doesn't come from what we wear or how we look, but from our hearts. If we fail to embrace this truth, we open the door for deep struggles with issues, like vanity, pride, and fear of rejection, which will affect our character.

When our value is rooted in who we are in Christ, we should be free from wrestling with fear and struggling with vanity and pride. Some may consider wearing makeup a gray area, but what part of a person does wearing decoration feed? Not humility, I would say.

True beauty is not something we can paint on or put on.

When I looked up the word *makeup* in the dictionary, I found all the entries were related to the use of cosmetics except when referring to a person's complete makeup or their total person, the "package" that is you or me. That led me to look up *cosmetics*:

1. A powder, lotion, lipstick, rouge, or other preparation for beautifying the face, skin, hair, nails, etc., and
2. Superficial measures to make something appear better, more attractive or more impressive.[44]

The definition of *cosmetics* lets us know that their use is solely to alter, change, or "improve" whatever they are applied to. As a creation of God, that implies a belief that by applying cosmetics, people can improve on what God made. That seems a bit presumptuous. **It saddens me that people think their estimation of beauty is more accurate or important than God's estimation.**

Let's look at the origin of the word *cosmetics*. It comes from the Greek word *kosmētikós* which means "relating to adornment, equivalent to *kosmēt (ós)* adorned, arranged (verbid of *kosmeîn,* derivative of *kósmos* order, arrangement)."[45]

You may have glossed over that bit because of the unfamiliar words, but I want you to notice something. The word *cosmetics* is derived from the same word as the root word of *cosmos*.

In *Covered by Love* we discussed divine order, and here we see it again. The Greek root word for both *cosmetics* and *cosmos* refers to order, form, and the harmonious arrangement of the world or universe. Girls, let's go with God's arrangement—from vast galaxies to the shape of our cheekbones and lips. We really are wonderful designs of the Master Creator, and we don't need to reorder what God ordered in our appearances.

Have you considered that it might displease God when we aren't satisfied with what He made, when we want to change His design? The Bible does say a believer is the "temple" of God (I Corinthians 3:16). We know we should never defile or deface God's temple. Here's the play on words: Don't change "de face" of God's temple—your face! The word *defile* also means "pollute." Pollution lessens value and gives a cheaper perception.

We choose how we present ourselves. **We aren't "do-it-yourself" projects,** like unfinished furniture bought to be "fixed up." It doesn't seem an honest approach to think that God gave us blank canvases or design-your-own bodies. He designed us! You don't need a makeover when God made you wonderful, marvelous, even!

Let's look at Esther for another biblical example on adornment. When Esther first approached the king, before she was chosen as queen, she did not enter the king's presence wearing a crown or fancy things of the world. It was only after her wedding that she gained access to the crown and all that came with it. We are the "betrothed," still waiting for that great day—our "coronation." While we are still in this world, our ornamentation should be like Esther's: grace, humility, and smelling good. We'll look at that more in Chapter 5.

Let's look at Queen Esther for a Bible lesson. She was a Hebrew girl forced into a "beauty contest" to see who would be the next queen of Persia. She didn't apply for the position. Her ancestors were prisoners of war. But Esther was selected and went to the king's house with the other girls where, we read in Esther 2:9, she received "things for purification." These "things," according to *Strong's Concordance*, refer to items used for rubbing and scraping[46]—those hygiene issues again. Her beauty treatments are detailed in Esther 2:12 as "six months with oil of myrrh, and six months with sweet odours, and with other things for the purifying of the women." We aren't talking about appearance-altering cosmetics but about being clean and smelling good. In verse 15, we read that Esther asked for nothing else than what was given her by the king's attendant. What happened when Esther went before the king? She "obtained favour in the sight of all them that looked upon her."

According to Maggie Angeloglou, the author of *A History of Make-up*, cosmetic use even today is a "charm against evil, as it was in the most primitive ages."[47] That might sound a bit far-fetched, but her basis is this: Cosmetics are used by a woman to "make herself complete" and their application switches a person from their safe home environment to their 'outdoor self.'"[48] She states that in our culture "the habit of making up is so deeply ingrained that many women feel ashamed and insecure without it," like "I'm not dressed."[49]

Is it possible to "paint on" or apply something externally that has the power to make a person truly complete? That we would feel like we have all our necessary parts, lacking nothing? It's such a superficial concept. **When Jesus comes into a person's life, the result is more than an external makeover. His internal renovation does the work of completion, filling lives with His goodness and beauty.**

Angeloglou believes "cosmetics are not only barriers, they are tribal codes." She's saying makeup creates a boundary of sorts, and it is also used to distinguish the group of people to which a person belongs. In the same way, not using makeup can also identify a person with a group of people or remove a barrier or boundary, revealing the real person to the world—unmasked.

In *A History of Make-up*, I discovered that cosmetics were first used in tribal warfare. Witch doctors disguised themselves with ritual paint to scare unseen forces. Some even used what is called a "devil mask," considered a "most necessary part of the witch doctor's equipment, which not only disguised him from evil and frightened human enemies, but kept his own community in a suitable state of awe."[50] War paint diminished as civilization progressed, but "cosmetics continued to have religious significance."[51]

Many consider Egyptians to be among the earliest users of face paint; however, the origins of Egyptian cosmetics have been traced to the Middle Stone Age. Egyptians developed their cosmetics worn for adornment and protection against the sun.

© Christopher Michel

The *bindi* or red mark traditionally worn only by Hindu females between their eyebrows is now worn by women from other faiths. This application is applied by those who believe it enhances beauty and protects against demons and bad luck and provides the ability to retain energy and strengthen concentration.[52] Did you notice that? Here is one more example of a spiritual connection with wearing makeup.

As I studied, some words seemed to jump off the pages and really got my attention. *A History of Make-up* is not a religious book but an educational-type text recording the development and use of cosmetics. One phrase I found was "a slash of poppy colour on the lips which was not completely honest." It made me stop and think, and that's good to do from time to time.

The observation that putting color on your lips is not being completely honest affirms the fact that |**makeup is a false appearance.**| We know the Lord doesn't like false things. Look up all the following: false witness (Exodus 20:16), false report (Exodus 23:1), false matter (Exodus 23:7), swear falsely (Leviticus 19:12), deal falsely (Leviticus 19:11), falsehood in general (II Samuel 18:13), and false prophets (Matthew 7:15). Did you know the Bible even talks about false brethren (Galatians 2:4) and false lips (Proverbs 17:4)? I know this last verse isn't talking about lipstick, but the irony made me smile.

The psalmist wrote that he hated "every false way" (Psalm 119:104). God loves truth. Why, the Bible tells us He *is* the truth—and the way (John 14:6). When we are walking with the Lord, we shouldn't walk in false ways, but true ways. That means a pure heart and a pure appearance.

In *A History of Make-up*, a reference to medieval faces said, "although their eyebrows are plucked they are innocent of cosmetics."[53] "Innocent of cosmetics" Hmmm. Could that mean wearing cosmetics perhaps displays

makeup is a false appearance

a lack of innocence? There are certainly many scriptural references to the painted woman that are not favorable. We'll look more at that, but in general, an "impudent" look (Proverbs 7:13) is not pleasing to the Lord. The words translated "impudent woman" can also mean "strong presence"—you know, that forward or bold look. Wearing cosmetics certainly creates a bolder look than a face "innocent" of them.

In the ancient Greek culture, respectable housewives did not wear make-up, but interestingly courtesans, not ladies, underwent extensive beauty treatments, and lower-level prostitutes liberally used colorful cosmetics. Men and women often married for political and social reasons but led separate lives from their spouses. Men would have courtesans for their pleasure but not as their wives or the mothers of their children. In today's language, a courtesan would be an escort or prostitute.

When Romans came to power, they plunged into a life of decadence and wealth they had not known before. They began using cosmetics and dyeing their hair. In 40 A.D. a law passed that required Roman prostitutes to dye their hair blonde. "Blonde hair became the brand of the prostitute." Of course, God made blonde hair, but this is the deal. It was abnormal for Romans to have blonde hair. They were attracted to and wanted something they didn't have.

Over time, Roman aristocrats decided they would like to have blonde hair and began wearing flaxen wigs. Eventually blonde hair became acceptable regardless of social ranking. But in the beginning those who first altered their normal appearance were immoral women. As years passed, reservations slipped, and what was once a mark of immorality became accepted among the general public.

During the time of the Roman Empire, Indian women developed their own art of using makeup as allurement or a way to attract men. Perhaps it's part of our base female need to feel secure. If we're desirable and attractive, we think we have a higher value. Don't let insecurity over your appearance lead you to adopt the ways started in pagan cultures by immoral women and that have now seeped into society at large. **Just because a majority is doing something, it doesn't make it right. Do what's right and pleasing to the Lord.**

In a sermon given in the twelfth or thirteenth century, a preacher declared women who powdered their faces to make themselves fair and seductive were "the devil's mousetrap, and their outer adornments are the treacherous cheese whereby many a mouse is enticed into the trap."[54] He called cosmetics "the devil's soap"[55] and gave this counsel to good men: "For God's sake keep yourselves from the devil's mousetrap."[56] And if I might add my own observation: Let's not be mousetraps, girls!

Angeloglou wrote, "Towards the end of the Middle Ages, the use of cosmetics had only been sponsored by notorious women."[57] "It is an interesting contradiction which recurs throughout social history that while harlots in high positions were reviled, they were also imitated."[58]

Let's move to the Middle Ages. In reference to a king's mistress, *A History of Makeup* reports, "Leaders of fashion were usually those women who would have been outcasts in a more humble or provincial society."[59] "The only other women who could dress and paint as they wished without condemnation were those of such superior birth that they would escape censure from their immediate circle and from the church."[60] It's clear from this quote the church did not approve of immodest dress or the use of makeup. **The people setting the fashion trends, even hundreds of years ago, were not respected ladies. Today the pattern continues.** The Proverbs 31 woman would probably not make the cover of any of today's women's magazines.

Cosmetics in the fourteenth century were often identified with witchcraft. Isabeau of Bavaria, the queen consort of France (1385–1422), used a lotion made of boar's brains, crocodile glands, and wolves' blood.[61] Yuck! We'll see more association between lotions and potions as we read on.

Who's the Fairest of Them All?

In the sixteenth century, women began using a product called "ceruse." Also known as "spirits of Saturn," this poisonous pigment was used as a skin whitener. It damaged skin, caused hair loss, and over time caused lead poisoning that could end in death. It was in great demand for almost two hundred years. Sadly, its use eventually devastated the health of European women.

During Elizabeth I's reign in England, an edict was issued against any woman who used, among other things, makeup and false hair. "The penalty was the same as that for witchcraft."[62] When she was twenty-nine, Queen Elizabeth suffered a devastating case of smallpox that left her scarred and bald—after which she began using cosmetics herself, a face paste made from lead and egg whites.

"Miracle lotions" made of refined mercury were used in hopes of eliminating spots, freckles, and warts. What was meant to beautify corroded a girl's flesh and caused her to lose her teeth early in life, leaving her a "rotting wreck" by the age of thirty.[63] The cause of Queen Elizabeth's death was never confirmed, but it was generally believed she died of blood poisoning that was likely the result of the makeup she wore to mask the marks smallpox left on her face.

Early English peddlers of cosmetics were classed as witches. They knew no woman of lower income would give up her precious money for a simple moisturizer or cream. They concocted "formulas" they promised would "rejuvenate," and "eliminate all scars."

106

Women have been sold fairytale promises that if they would "wear this" or "put on that," their lives would be better. Firm. Lift. Invigorate. Enhance. Improve. Accentuate. Tingle. Glow. Why, using cosmetics can do all sorts of wonders! It can make an older person feel young again or make a common girl feel like a cover girl if you'll just spend your money on cosmetics and creams. We may laugh at the women who bought the old peddlers' potions, but are we really far removed from the same type of quackery in the cosmetic industry? They use "science" to back up their advertising statements, but today's modern makeup claims are closer to science fiction than actual fountain of youth discoveries.

We're still in England, and it's 1837. Victoria has taken the throne, and the morals of the royal court were lower than the devil's toe jam. Previous generations of the royal family had been guilty of almost every sin possible. I won't give the long list. Just trust me on this one.

In response to the shameless immorality of their predecessors, Queen Victoria, along with her husband, Albert, made a deliberate turn. They veered in a Puritan-style reaction that spawned the Victorian Era. Victoria and Albert's influence gave their subjects a positive example of faithful marriage and close family life. Things changed so dramatically that court attendants no longer used cosmetics due to new moral modesty promoted by their "innocent" queen. Only cologne was allowed, and wearing "rouge" was considered to make a person immoral or peculiar.

The Elizabethan and Victorian eras were forever ago and oceans away. Let's look at some more contemporary and close-to-home examples. We will have to step back a moment to move forward with this tale.

In the year of our Lord 1620, Puritans traveled from England to establish a new colony across the ocean blue. The United States of America was founded on the principles of these pilgrims, moral purists who believed mankind existed for the glory of God and shunned outer adornments. Puritan beliefs, along with the rugged lifestyle required of early American settlers, resulted in a lack of cosmetic use that continued throughout the 1800s.

Nellie Steward, an actress in 1908 and quoted in *A History of Makeup*, said "Makeup was used exclusively for stage purposes,"[64] and that actresses were the only women who knew anything about using cosmetics or "would dare to be seen in public wearing anything but the lightest film of rice powder which was used to whiten complexions, the current standard of beauty. It created a whitewashed look and caused swollen, enlarged pores."[65]

As the film industry developed, the use of makeup became more widely accepted. According to Angeloglou, "The growing acceptance of cosmetics, was, initially, because of the cinema." Famous actress Theda Bara, considered the first sex symbol of the movies, caused "a minor revolution" in makeup—her "real face heavily disguised by Helena Rubenstein."[66]

Petroleum alcohol, a main ingredient used in cosmetics, was diverted to war supply in the 1940s causing a big boom in cosmetic use after World War II. When Technicolor introduced colored motion pictures, a desire arose among the public to match what the stars were wearing. Max Factor created "makeup for the stars" and every product was designed with a purpose. For instance, glossy lips were meant to give an eager, just-licked appearance.

The beauty industry played on women's fears of being undesirable and on their longings to be beautiful. They convinced women that lipstick could raise them from inferiority. Elizabeth Arden, founder of a cosmetics empire, said, "I judge a woman and a horse by the same criteria: legs, head and rear end."[67] They set the standards in their day and their companies are doing the same even now. I want to encourage you and let you know that **you don't have to look like someone else's "model" of beauty. Instead, be a "role model," exemplifying true, inner, and everlasting beauty.**

Today, many women wear makeup because the marketing and use of cosmetics by others makes them feel less than "polished" in their public presentations. In *A History of Makeup*, Angeloglou wrote that "more and more products are aimed at a market in which women are uneasy and ashamed, conscious that they are not quite as perfect as the mirror for affluent living suggests."[68] Are we reflecting a sincere image? We need to look into the true mirror, the Word of God!

The most telling aspect of our lives—one that reveals the maturity and depth of our relationships with God—is not our outer appearance, but our inner desires. If my desire is to be close to the Lord, I will be close to His Word.

> It's impossible to draw closer to God and step away from His Word. They reside together in the Holy Place of His presence.

It is in the Word we find two important questions: 1) Who are we to talk back to God? and 2) Should we say to the one who formed us, "Why did You make me like this?" (See Romans 9:20.) It looks like it's not a good idea to talk back to God or question His work.

Whoa, Max—Stand Down!

Here is a little illustration I hope you will enjoy. Imagine you are Adam. You are just waking up in the Garden of Eden after a long sleep. God says He has something special for you. It's a surprise! Across the clearing you see her. She's making her way toward you. Your heart rate picks up. Your eyes are blinking in wonder and disbelief at this gorgeous chick heading your way.

Before Eve approaches, another man rushes out of the bushes. He has a case in one hand. "Stop! Stop, right there!" he commands Eve. And then this man (his name is Max Factor) opens his case.

"No offense, God," Max says. "You did a pretty good job, but I have some things here that can make what you did even better." Max whips out a brush and applies some red to the tip before approaching Eve. "I'll just darken these lips and then her cheeks. I'll define her eyelids a bit."

Now that may sound silly, but isn't that, in essence, what people are doing when they paint what God has designed, constructed in the womb and brought to life?

Is the Fox Watching the Hen House?

Let's look at another feature of the cosmetics industry. We've touched on some of the physical harm done in the past. People may believe that with current regulations they are safe to use whatever products are in the marketplace. In the United States, the Food and Drug Administration regulates things taken orally but does not control the manufacture and distribution of cosmetics that are absorbed by human bodies through the skin. Instead, this industry is regulated by a group it created: the Cosmetic Ingredient Review (CIR).

The CIR is funded and directed by the Personal Care Products Council. According to the Cosmetic Ingredient Review, it is overseeing itself in a business that generates $250 billion a year.

To some, the idea of makeup being anything less than normal and acceptable in our society may be a new concept. That's understandable. Not everyone was raised in a home or church that uses the Bible as a handbook for life as their basis for what's acceptable over what culture condones. Once we are blessed to understand the treasures in the Bible, **for a committed Christian the Word of God should always trump the message of the world!**

A verse I would like to share with those who grew up with solid biblical teaching is II Timothy 3:15. From the *Amplified Bible*: "From your childhood you have had a knowledge of and been acquainted with the sacred Writings, which are able to instruct you and give you the understanding for salvation which comes through faith in Christ Jesus [through the leaning of the entire human personality on God in Christ Jesus in absolute trust and confidence in His power, wisdom, and goodness]."

You are blessed if you are acquainted with "the sacred Writings." They are able to instruct you and give you understanding. They show us the best way to live. If you were raised in a church that promotes godly, holy living, celebrate the goodness of God who made you with purpose and destiny.

If this is all new to you, then I encourage you to grab hold of this verse: "Thy hands have made me and fashioned me: give me understanding, that I may learn thy commandments" (Psalm 119:73).

You are God's creation and design. Think of it this way: Imagine you had a bug collection, and there were some fantastic moths among your carefully selected specimens, but your little sister decided to get out her paint-by-number set and re-color them. How would that make you feel? What if it was God, who made you, and you got out the paints and changed what He designed? How could that be pleasing to Him?

We aren't talking about hygiene, keeping clean and neat. We are discussing the use of colorful cosmetics that alter our God-given appearances. We don't change the look of other living creatures. Most people don't paint their pets. Some have, but it surely doesn't look natural. Have you ever seen a hot-pink poodle? That's just weird. What living things are painted? Horses? Fish? Guinea pigs? Trees? Flowers?

God made you beautiful. Just look at this: "Our sons [are] as plants, Becoming great in their youth, Our daughters as hewn stones, Polished—the likeness of a palace" (Psalm 144:12, YLT).[69] Wow. God's girls are like polished stones in a palace. That's pretty special. Do you know it would be a shame to paint marble or granite? It would hide beauty, not improve it. The Bible says followers of Jesus are like lively stones (I Peter 2:5). Why would you want to paint stonework? How would your mom like it if you painted her granite countertop or marble floor?

The Queen of Maybelline (C'est Moi—or, "It's Me")

I used to be what I have dubbed the "Queen of Maybelline." I knew how to apply makeup. I was very good at it. Let's travel back to the 80s, that period in history when people didn't just "accessorize," they "excess-orized." It was all about *big*—big hair, press-on fingernails, huge bows on the top of heads and backs of dresses, puffed sleeves (that Princess Di wedding look), eye-popping metallic and fluorescent-colored clothes, and lots and lots of makeup.

I was skillful at applying makeup and taught people how to do it themselves. I did stage makeup for a local community theater. Makeup was a very big part of my life as a teenager and young adult.

I remember when the Lord asked me to lay it aside for Him. It wasn't easy. I was an executive secretary in a professional work environment. I wrestled with His will with several days of fasting, prayer, and Bible study. I knew what God wanted from me. I didn't want to give it up, but I couldn't say "no" to Jesus.

The first day I arrived at work without my artfully decorated face, people looked at me like something was wrong. Did somebody die? Are you sick? I don't remember what my specific answer was to the woman who asked the questions, but I can tell you her reaction was not encouraging. She actually seemed rather "put off" with my decision, but I reminded myself she was not a spiritually-minded person and tried to shake off the negative vibes flowing my way.

A couple of weeks passed and I was called into a meeting with the human resources manager. He told me my co-worker was trying to get me fired—that I no longer looked "professional." Honestly, I didn't feel I looked professional or pretty. I remember walking into the bathroom and seeing this person across the room who appeared frighteningly pale and plain—and then realizing it was *my* reflection in the mirror. That was the worst of it, though. I wasn't fired. My skin actually improved once I stopped daily applying pore-clogging foundation, colors, and powders. I learned to like the face God gave me.

There are some things we just have to learn, and contentment can be one of those things. (See Philippians 4:11.) You know what? I'm free and happy to be me, and I hope you learn to be happy being you.

Yes, I know what it's like to have blonde eyelashes and think, "Just a little mascara would help them show up better." I understand. But if I believe wearing a lot of makeup isn't pleasing because it alters the face God gave me, then my wearing a little couldn't be pleasing either—unless, of course, I'm trying to please myself.

My Testimony

When the Lord began dealing with me about consecration issues, I wasn't really happy about it. Nope. I was content where I was. I had a real relationship with God that was born of faith that led me to repentance, baptism in the name of Jesus Christ, and the infilling of the Holy Ghost. I was a worship leader. I was involved in prison ministry. I was content.

Most toddlers love being home with their parents. They are happy and secure. There comes a time when they move from diapers to potty, then to kindergarten, then to elementary school, and all the way to whatever level of higher learning they reach. A toddler isn't expected to know things like thermodynamic potentials or how to calculate the square root of a non-negative number. (Oh, my, I hope I don't have to know those either!) They just need to follow the instructions they are given and apply themselves to learning and growing.

So, I was happy where I was, just celebrating my new faith. God was good. Life was good. But He had more for me. I just didn't know it. Through a friend, I visited a church that taught and exemplified principles of consecration that we've discussed throughout *The Pure Path Series*. They had the same doctrine on the Godhead and baptism. The same Spirit that filled me, filled them—but there was something different about them. There was a liberty and freedom in worship I didn't know anything about. Yes, I had been happy in my toddler-hood at the other church, but the Lord wanted me to grow and experience more of Him. It wasn't easy, but I knew I had to do it, and I have never regretted that decision.

I'm not saying I've never looked in the mirror and wished things looked different. Every lady, young or old, has days she just doesn't feel good about her appearance. I was sorry to leave my friends and church family that had introduced me to the Lord, but my allegiance had to be to my Savior and to what He had revealed to me. Guess what? Now I experience that liberty and power and joy for myself. It's worth it, girls!

I'm not dissing anyone's walk with God, but I've found that THE MORE YOU GIVE HIM, THE MORE HIM HE GIVES YOU. God has always honored obedience, more so even than sacrifice (I Samuel 15:22).

We can always come up with some kind of argument to twist Scripture. The *Amplified Bible* says not to be deceived with "empty excuses and groundless arguments" (Ephesians 5:6).

What Does the Bible Say— Specifically?

So far we've looked at Scripture, history, illustrations, and a couple of testimonies. Let's dig a bit deeper into the Bible. One thing I've never found in my research is a single verse of Scripture that portrayed wearing makeup in a favorable light. What I did discover was that in the Bible, **cosmetic use was almost always associated with sexual immorality.**

I'll do my best to be discreet and tactful, but we're going to dive into a subject that might make some a bit uncomfortable. Before we look at our next Bible verse, let me set the scene. In this verse, the Lord is speaking to Israel in a symbolic conversation. God's people had rejected the Lord as husband by committing spiritual adultery.

I know we don't usually read the *New Living Translation*, but I just had to share this with you to help you understand the meaning of these words.

"But now bring charges against Israel—your mother—for she is no longer my wife, and I am no longer her husband. Tell her to remove the prostitute's makeup from her face and the clothing that exposes her breasts" (Hosea 2:2, NLT).[70] What does this verse have to do with makeup?

Several translations of this verse talk about Israel putting away "whoredoms," prostitutions, and unfaithfulness "out of her sight"—or "from her face." What's the connection between immorality and the face? *Jamieson-Fausset Brown Bible Commentary* says, the words in the *King James Version* translated "out of her sight" might rather mean "'from her face.' Her very countenance unblushingly betrayed her lust, as did also her exposed 'breasts.'"[71]

Our faces reveal so much. In *Barnes' Notes on the Bible* we read the words "out of her sight" are "literally 'from her face.' The face is the seat of modesty, shame or shamelessness."[72]

Let's recap. In this verse, we have unfaithfulness, idolatry, and face painting intertwining. Go down a few verses in the same chapter and we see things aren't looking too good for this "wife." She was punished for idolatry, unfaithfulness, and decking herself with rings and jewelry (Hosea 2:13).

The Bible speaks of wearing makeup as "painting." The first person many Christians think of when we begin the discussion of makeup is Queen Jezebel. Makeup didn't make Jezebel a wicked queen, but she was wicked, there's no doubt about that. She was a pagan who had hundreds of God's prophets put to death. Sweet? No way!

In II Kings 9:30 the Bible lets us know that when Jezebel saw Jehu, a commander in the Israelite army and the new king of Israel, coming toward the city, she put on makeup and arranged her hair. She knew he was coming after her, so she dolled up and then stood in the window hoping to appeal to Jehu with her looks. Can't you just see her striking a pose with lowered lids and pouty lips?

It seems obvious she was hoping to seduce Jehu and save herself, and she used makeup in her efforts. Proverbs 6:25 reads, "Lust not after her beauty in thine heart; neither let her take thee with her eyelids." This verse, although not specifically talking about eye makeup, does reinforce the fact that eye signals indicate sexual interest. Eye makeup is worn to draw attention to the eyes—a blinking marquis to make sure those who pass by get the message.

Let's read Jeremiah 4:30 from *The Message*: "And you, what do you think you're up to? Dressing up in party clothes, decking yourselves out in jewelry, putting on lipstick and rouge and mascara! Your primping goes for nothing. You're not going to seduce anyone."[73]

Seduction was the motivator behind the actions being taken in this verse of Scripture. Yes, makeup and jewelry can, in the eyes of some, enhance "prettiness" in a sensual way. Sparkling and tinkling and shining adornments are commercials that beckon, "I'm special. Pick me."

You may have looked and found no Scripture verse that says, "Thou shalt not paint thy face." Does that mean it's acceptable? The answer is not what this pastor or that pastor thinks, or what my girlfriend thinks, or what I think! The most important opinion comes from God, and the most important question we can ask will always be, "Is this pleasing to the Lord?"

That is a much better question than, "What can I get by with and still make it to Heaven?" **If we read in Scripture examples of activities or practices that displease the Lord, or are associated with immorality, that should be the end of any mental or spiritual argument.** With a heart to please God, Christian standards are not burdens to bear but tokens of our love!

God wants His people motivated and led by love for Him. He says He will guide us with His eye. What He sees should be what we see. When He gives a loving glance indicating the path we should take, or even a correction, how should we respond? Should we act like horses or mules that have no understanding and have to be led with bits and bridles? (See Psalm 32:8-9.)

Ask any parent and I'm sure they will agree, they would much prefer their children correct themselves after getting "the look." I find no joy, no pleasure, in correcting my children when they choose to misbehave. "I have no greater joy than to hear that my children walk in truth" (III John 4).

|Sincere Christians will want to keep every aspect of their lives

in harmony with God's revealed will. | Their motivation will stem from their love, reverence, and respect for God.

Let's look for some more specific insight on colorful cosmetics. In the Old Testament, when God's people were backslidden, they were described collectively as a harlot or unfaithful wife. Let's look in Ezekiel for an example. In chapter 23, verse 4, the two "women" in the passage are actually two cities, Samaria and Jerusalem. Later in the chapter, the Lord speaks of His displeasure in their behavior:

"They even sent messengers for men who came from far away, and when they arrived you bathed yourself for them, applied eye makeup and put on your jewelry. You sat on an elegant couch, with a table spread before it on which you had placed the incense and olive oil that belonged to me. The noise of a carefree crowd was around her; drunkards were brought from the desert along with men from the rabble, and they put bracelets on the wrists of the woman and her sister and beautiful crowns on their heads. Then I said about the one worn out by adultery, 'Now let them use her as a prostitute, for that is all she is.' And they slept with her. As men sleep with a prostitute, so they slept with those lewd women, Oholah and Oholibah" (Ezekiel 23:40-44, NIV).

These women painted their faces and put on jewelry to attract others and lure them into sin. Eye makeup was used to make the eyes look large and passionate, but was not commonly practiced among holy women in the Old and New Testaments. *Calmut's Dictionary of the Holy Bible* records, "As it is not customary among us for women to paint their eyelids particularly, we do not usually perceive the full import of the expressions in Scripture referring to this custom."[74] He was saying that since Christian women in his time (1830) didn't wear eye makeup, people might miss the importance of the biblical references to the practice.

I believe there is a flip-side to that coin. If something is adopted as a common practice in society, the significance of the Scriptures on that practice may also be missed. We can easily gloss over things in the Bible if we think they don't relate to our time and culture. That's why it's important to "rightly [divide] the word of truth" (II Timothy 2:15) based on solid biblical principles and not the common practice or thought of contemporary society.

Let's look at Jezebel again. *Calmut's* gives us the literal meaning of what the *King James* in II Kings 9:30 translates "she painted her face." It meant that "she formed a streak of black upon them, thereby, apparently enlarging the eyes, and rendering their effect more powerful."[75]

This practice of using eyeliner is also referred to in Ezekiel 23:40. *E.D. Smith's Bible Dictionary* defines it: "A small probe of wood, ivory or silver is wet with rose-water and dipped in an impalpable black powder, and is then drawn between the lids of the eye nearly closed, and leaves a narrow black border, which is thought a great ornament."[76]

Calmut's explains the meaning of Jeremiah 4:30 in the *King James*, "though thou rentest thy face with painting," as "though thou cause thine eye-lids to seem to be starting out of thine head, through the strength of thy black paint which is applied to them, yet shall the decoration be in vain."

In Proverbs 6:25, we read, "Lust not after her beauty in thine heart; neither let her take thee with her eyelids." It would be silly to think someone could be captured by eyelids. This is referring to the effect of the eyelids after "which she has rendered so large and brilliant by the assistance of art, as to enchant beholders."[77]

Although the use of paint as a cosmetic was and is practiced in ancient and modern eastern cultures, *Smith's Bible Dictionary* lets us know, "It does not appear, however, to have been by any means universal among the Hebrews."[78] *Smith's* mentions that the references to Hebrew women applying paint as cosmetics "are few; and in each instance it seems to have been used as meretricious art, unworthy of a woman of high character."[79] Wow!

123

Mr. Smith knew some highfalutin words. I had to look up *meretricious* in the dictionary. It means:

1. alluring by a show of flashy or vulgar attractions; tawdry,
2. based on pretense, deception, or insincerity, or
3. pertaining to or characteristic of a prostitute.[80]

None of that sounds like anything I want people thinking about when they look at me.

This reminded me of a Lutheran pamphlet on cosmetics someone gave me. It contained an article advising exchange students to avoid wearing lipstick. If they chose to wear lipstick, they could be mistaken for prostitutes. In the same pamphlet, a Chinese missionary reported that where he worked the only "women who painted their faces, wore ear rings, and had long painted fingernails" were prostitutes.

In 1770 a bill was introduced in British Parliament that actually outlawed the use of makeup.[81] It wasn't so long ago that in our country and other predominantly Christian nations, wearing makeup was the exception, not the rule.

When did women in our culture begin using cosmetics? In the early days of Hollywood. I am not "calling names" to slur anyone, but it's clear the starlets of the film industry were ungodly and adulterous women. For some reason, our nation has allowed the women of the big screen to set the standard for society.

| **A made-up face has never been a symbol of godliness or purity.** |
Consider this: When is the last time you saw a modest, unadorned woman advertising a casino, cigarettes, alcohol, or some other vice?

Wearing makeup could well be considered a "mark of the world." There is supposed to be a difference between the look of the world and the look of the Lord's beloved.

Let's see what the New Testament has to say. In I Timothy 2:9, when Paul used the word *shamefacedness* to address how women should present themselves, he wasn't talking about scowling. That's a word that means to show respect, reverence, self-restraint, and modesty. In Scripture, and throughout history, makeup has been used to play up sensuality in women and arouse desire in men. **The Bible always associates the use of makeup with brazenness, seduction, and prostitution.** These aren't my conclusions but the true record according to the Word of God.

From the Top of Your Head, to the Tips of Your Nails

It seems logical that if we aren't to use false colors on our faces, the same would apply to the tips of our fingers, our toenails, and tops of our heads—and for all the same reasons. A friend told me that as she began to gray, she struggled with wanting to dye her hair. It's easy to make the argument that it's not really changing the color, it's just bringing back the original, God-chosen color. Right? Hmmm.

Natural hair color is determined by the number and shape of melanin granules in the hair. If a person dyes their hair, it doesn't change the melanin. It just masks the color for a time. She said the Lord gave her a direct answer when she was praying. She was reminded of Matthew 5:36, where Jesus said a person can't make one hair white or black. She thought, "Oh, yes, we can. We now have Lady Clairol." The fact is, you can only dye the hair from the scalp outward, but at the root the color is changing to gray. When you dye your hair, you are defying Gods choice for the color of your hair.

The need for repeated treatments traps people in an unending cycle that proves they are defying God's design. It's almost as if you are constantly arguing with and trying to outdo God! It's also one more vanity "trap" that demands time, attention, and resources. A person may consider the choice to dye their hair the color of their choice. But the truth of your real hair color will become visible—may I say "uprooted"—if you don't keep up with the constant demand for maintenance.

|You are a limited edition, one-of-a-kind special, designer version of you.| When a consecrated, Spirit-filled person enters a public place and the light of the Holy Ghost shines through them, it can make people around them uncomfortable. The people being made uncomfortable by the presence of the Holy Ghost will often pressure the believer to "dim" their light.

When you hear a statement like, "You would look so beautiful with just a little makeup," realize it may be an attempt to dim your light and convince you to conform—so that it makes them more comfortable. If you are dealing with someone who is not spiritually minded, you really don't need to go into a lot of detail about the choices you have made to please God. Instead of focusing on issues of consecration, talk to them about the love, hope, joy, and peace of God. If they don't have a relationship with Him, they are not going to understand your godly choices.

It's amazing, if we really stop and think about it, how many people feel they can't go out in public until they "put on their faces." My friend, God put on your face, and He likes it (Genesis 1:31)!

"I will praise thee; for I am fearfully and wonderfully made: marvellous are thy works; and that my soul knoweth right well" (Psalm 139:14). This verse seems to say that **when a person lives content with the way God made them, marveling at His wonderful creative work, their life becomes an offering of praise to their Creator.**

Consider a couple of questions: How do you feel God would prefer that you present yourself in public? How do you believe God would prefer that you present yourself before Him?

"The sinless One took on the face of a sinner
so that we sinners could take on
the face of a saint."
— Max Lucado

Chapter Five

Redefining and Reclaiming Beauty

Redefining and Reclaiming Beauty

Everyone wants to feel good about themselves; that is a very natural and normal desire. I do want you to know that what is displayed as "ideal beauty" in magazines and on billboards is not a true reflection of normal, healthy women. We would be hard-pressed to find images in the media that haven't been digitally manipulated.

What difference does this make to you and me? | **The media-portrayed "ideal" isn't real.** | Proportions are distorted. Eyes are enlarged. Hips are minimized. Cheekbones are lifted. Lips are plumped. Necks and legs are elongated—and the list goes on! It's not normal or natural for women to look like most of the images we see in advertising. An advertiser will distort a model's natural appearance to convince people like you and me that we aren't quite up to par. We "need" to purchase their products in order to be what they consider beautiful. Hmmm. Seems a bit self-serving, don't you agree?

It's no wonder the digitally-altered faces and bodies we see in media inspire people to go to extremes to meet unreal standards. The beauty industry wants you to believe the distance between your pathetic reality and their stunning, desirable ideal can be vaulted with the pole of your pocketbook.

> "To be yourself in a world that is constantly trying to make you something else is the greatest accomplishment."
> – Ralph Waldo Emerson

| **You are so much more than "eye candy."** | Your value is not determined by what you look like, but by the "total person" package.

It's unbelievable how much people spend in time and money to live up to an illusion. Happiness, love, and success are not the results of cosmetics, surgeries, or what we dangle from our appendages. I'm not downplaying the need for hygiene or how wonderful a pedicure or massage feels. We are talking about things beyond occasional pampering.

The sad truth is that through media, people are lied to every day in the messages they see, hear, and read in order to manipulate their insecurities for corporate profits. That might sound harsh, but Charles Revson, the founder of Revlon, once called the beauty business the selling of "hope in a jar."

Let's untwist the twisted message and put pretty back into perspective. Wouldn't it be wonderful if people could grasp the true meaning of beauty rather than accept what we've been fed by profiteering opportunists?

When it comes to body shape, there's a deep instinctive reason guys are attracted to curves. God put the desire in men to be attracted to that image. It's normal. What's not normal is the Barbie image and the unreasonable expectation that every woman should look a certain way and stay that way for life. It's the longing to stay desirable that inspires women to try to look forever like "the perfect mate."

"Mimicry is the goal of the beauty industry."
– Nancy Etcoff, author of *Survival of the Prettiest*

Considering the "perfect mate" concept, let's look at an article, "Pots of Promise," from *The Economist,* a London-based newspaper that claims to offer "in-depth analysis and intelligent insight on the latest issues."

"Long lustrous hair has always been a sign of good health; mascara makes eyes look bigger and younger; blusher and red lipstick mimic signs of sexual arousal. Whatever the culture … flawless skin is seen as a testament to both youth and health."[82]

There's a saying these days. It's not one of my favorites, but I think it applies here: "It is what it is." Cosmetics were created to give an illusion or enhance the perception that the person wearing them is healthy, fit, and ready to mate. The next girl you pass on the sidewalk may not know the reason behind what she is doing, but it goes back to that deep, instinctive drive in the heart of most every woman. In her beauty, she is desirable, and that creates security for her.

As Christians, we need to know our security rests entirely in God. When I was only thirty-two years old, a stay-at-home mom of two small children, I lost my husband to cancer. Before he unexpectedly fell to the floor with a collapsed spinal column, I was certain my future was all set. God had blessed me with a good man who had a great job and who loved me.

In one moment what I expected my life to be unalterably changed. My story isn't unique. Accidents happen. Thieves steal. Companies close. Economies turn. Our security isn't in our education, our spouses, or anything else we might consider our "safety nets." Our security is in God (Psalm 62).

When we realize this, we can have peace and confidence in who we are. As we embrace the reality of our unique beauty, the total package God made us to be, we realize we may never look like those around us who turn to products and treatments to "enhance" their appearances. Of course, there's no way we will look like the ladies on the billboards and magazine covers, but that's OK. We are advertisements of a different sort. As we wear our God-given faces and bodies with joyful smiles and confidence, we are walking advertisements for the kingdom of God. And the kingdom of God isn't about "meat and drink"—in other words, the things of this world. It's about righteousness, peace, and joy.

Revsen was wrong. **We can't purchase jars of hope. Jesus purchased hope and gave it to His followers** (John 14:27). You and I are earthen vessels that have the privilege of dispensing true hope in a world where so many are searching for something real.

Sharrie Williams, great niece of Maybelline's founder, wrote a book about growing up in the Williams family. In *The Maybelline Story* she shares: "I believed that because of the perfection that was demanded in our family, I was more of a mannequin than a real person." I could add comments here, but let her words sink in. "I was more of a mannequin than a real person." Why? Because of the so-called "perfection" that was demanded of her family by the cosmetic business.

There are moments in our lives when we decide to "draw our lines" and say, "That's enough." I hope the reading of this book has fostered that in you. What pain have you experienced in the name of beauty? What have you spent? Have you ever starved yourself or binged or purged because your body didn't look like you wanted? Have you ever felt like you didn't measure up because you didn't look a certain way? It's time to say, "Enough!" Realize that **beauty isn't what you look like, but who you are** (Proverbs 31). **You don't "wear" beauty. You are a beauty!**

That doesn't mean God is finished with us. The Lord continues to work in

You don't "wear" beauty. You ARE a beauty!

our lives. When He's working, it doesn't cause physical pain but changes us deep in the core of who we are. C.S. Lewis explained it this way in his famous book, *Mere Christianity*:

"Imagine yourself as a living house. God comes in to rebuild that house. At first, perhaps, you can understand what He is doing. He is getting the drains right and stopping the leaks in the roof and so on; you knew that those jobs needed doing and so you are not surprised. But presently He starts knocking the house about in a way that does not seem to make any sense. What on earth is He up to? The explanation is that He is building quite a different house from the one you thought of—throwing out a new wing here, putting on an extra floor there, running up towers, making courtyards. You thought you were being made into a comfortable little cottage: but He is building a palace. He intends to come and live in it Himself."[83]

I hope you will always remember that a relationship with Jesus isn't about following rules; it's about falling in love with the One who wrote the rules for your blessing and protection. Sometimes we get so caught up in the question of "Is it right or wrong?" that we lose sight of an even more important question: | **"Is it pleasing to God?"** | When I was converted, I always went to my pastor with questions when there was something I wasn't sure of, to see it was wrong for me. He gave me an answer that has stayed with me, and I have taught it to others. He stated, "If you feel you need to ask if it is right or wrong, then that is your conscience speaking to you about giving it up." Paul stated it this way: "Herein do I exercise myself, to have always a conscience void of offence toward God, and toward men" (Acts 24:16).

Paul had previously taught the church in Corinth the principle of Christian liberty as it applies to things that are neither good nor bad in character. The Corinthians, however, used this general truth to follow the deviant teachings of the Epicureans. Paul was saying that **even if everything is lawful in a strict sense of the law, all things aren't profitable or beneficial.** (See I Corinthians 6:12.)

Think about this: You could choose today to watch a R-rated movie filled with profanity and steamy sex scenes. Would that be a good choice? Take a minute and answer the question, "Why or why not?" If your answers were similar to mine, I think they would also apply to wearing outer adornment. What do you think?

Satan seems to have a special ability to convince people that rebellion and disobedience are not rebellion and disobedience. He introduces his schemes to steal, kill, and destroy as "enlightenment" or "new revelations." If the devil is talking, what is he doing? He's lying! So what are the wicked intentions of this deceiver? Come on and say it with me: rebellion and disobedience.

You and I are God's "good" handiwork! Body modifications or artwork, applied either temporarily or permanently, say "I can improve on what God made!" The very term "modification" means change. Your unique shape, look, coloring, and features were designed by God; and what He makes, He considers good. I may wish I had someone else's long, dark eyelashes, but that doesn't mean I should feel at liberty to change the "me" God made so that I can look like someone else He made. Instead of comparing and changing, it would be nice if we appreciated individual beauty and learned to be content with what God gave us. Comparing isn't wise, you know. (See II Corinthians 10:12.) **If we're going to compare ourselves with something, it shouldn't be to other people, but to the Word of God.**

Contentment doesn't always come natural, but the apostle Paul taught us it could be "learned" (Philippians 4:11). He instructed his young disciple, Timothy, that "godliness with contentment is great gain" (I Timothy 6:6). That's a simple formula: **Godliness + Contentment = Great Gain.**

Godliness
+
Contentment
=
Great Gain

I like all three of those! Sign me up! The *Amplified Bible* describes contentment as "that contentment which is a sense of inward sufficiency." Deep in your "knower," you know God made you, and you know that is the reason you are A-OK. Our "sufficiency" is of God (II Corinthians 3:5) and we are "complete in him" (Colossians 2:10).

Wouldn't it be awesome if we had such a tremendous revival and release of revelation that people from all walks of life would fill our churches? I'd love to see the tattooed, the pierced, and the made up "lost" in worship—unshackled and redeemed!

May those who know the Lord but never understood the blessings in living set apart lives receive understanding and choose to live a dedicated, consecrated life unto the Lord. And yes, oh yes, may those who once knew and walked away—ones who might be afraid to come "home" with the marks of their choices forever on their bodies—return! And when they do, please, let's make everyone feel welcome in the house of the Lord! We have all fallen short. There is no perfect person. My marks and your marks may not be visible to the human eye but that doesn't mean we haven't tripped up and needed God's forgiveness over and over and over again.

One of my favorite Scripture verses is Micah 6:8. What a better world we would live in if we followed the *requirements* of God to do three simple things: 1) do justly, 2) love mercy, and 3) walk humbly with our God.

Remember, when it comes to new believers, being spiritually born doesn't mean a person is spiritually mature. We can't look at people who don't yet know biblical teachings on consecration issues and compare their spirituality with those who do.

The focus you and I need to maintain is on our own Christian growth and developing spiritual maturity. Spiritual fruit is a sign of maturity, not new life. A young tree doesn't bear fruit, but it is, without a doubt, a living plant.

Here's a great verse of Scripture on the subject: "Therefore let us leave the elementary teachings about Christ and go on to maturity" (Hebrews 6:1, NIV). To assist in this, God gave teachers to the church "for the perfecting of the saints" (Ephesians 4:11-12). Listen to the teachers God has placed in your life— even the teaching you receive as you read this book. We can't walk away from what we know and expect to walk in God's blessings.

If we want true spiritual liberty, we cannot liberate ourselves from God's call to holiness. If we desire maturity, we must learn to say no to our flesh. If we feed the carnal, it will grow and become stronger and take the lead. I want to give the lead to the eternal part of me, not the part that will one day perish.

We are souls living within earthly containers. What material did God use to make Adam? You know the answer: dirt! All we are—heart, soul, mind, and strength—is a gift from God. What will we give back to Him? We can only give that over which we have control. Our spirit was given by and belongs to God (Ecclesiastes 12:7). What we do have control over is our body and our mind.

I present my spirit to God and by His grace He renews me. I am called to control my thoughts and actions. We must learn to untangle our spirits from our flesh, and that's only possible when we choose to starve the sensory demands of our lower nature.

The kingdom of God is within us! If we allow our flesh to rule, we can lose that precious leading and guiding of the Holy Spirit, our communication with God. I want my life to bring glory to Him—body and spirit. They both belong to Him (I Corinthians 6:20).

So what's our focus to be? My focus is my Christian walk, and I pray yours is, or will be, also. Here are some questions we can ask ourselves on the subject of adornment:

- Could my choice to wear cosmetics or jewelry, or have a body modification done, present a temptation to someone else to sin?
- Is what I'm putting on functional for me or beneficial to others?
- Is too much of my time, attention, or resources going to the way I look on the outside?
- Does the way I present my body bring glory to God's creation (me) or the Creator (God)?
- Are my life choices on physical appearance in agreement with biblical teachings?
- Are my motives pure, for the good of others, or for my own pleasure?
- Do the items I buy show good stewardship, or am I wasting resources on a bunch of vanity-oriented "stuff"?

"Take this rule: whatever weakens your reason, impairs the tenderness of your conscience, obscures your sense of God, or takes off your relish of spiritual things; in short, whatever increases the strength and authority of your body over your mind, that thing is sin to you, however innocent it may be in itself."
— Susanna Wesley (Letter, June 8, 1725)

Work It Out!

We live in a space between two worlds. We must be careful not to cling to the physical world or we can lose the spiritual. But if we cling to the spiritual, we will have joy in both.

Don't give in! Resist anything that is strengthening your physical person's influence over your spiritual person. Be strong! Be courageous! And remember, | **when in doubt, do without!** | The apostle Paul has something to say to us: "Continue to work out your salvation with fear and trembling, for it is God who works in you to will and to act according to his good purpose. Do everything without complaining or arguing, so that you may become blameless and pure, children of God without fault in a crooked and depraved generation, in which you shine like stars in the universe" (Philippians 2:12-15, NIV).

The pressure to be attractive is intense; but remember, with every temptation there is a way to escape (I Corinthians 10:13). The Bible tells us to run in the opposite direction of youthful lusts (II Timothy 2:22). Even not-so-young people can still be tempted by youthful lusts, especially those who never "grew up."

Moderation—Yes, Again!

We've talked a lot about moderation. I want to re-emphasize that **"moderation" only applies to things that aren't specifically addressed in the Bible.** We can't be moderately faithful. It's impossible to be moderately honest.

And think about this bit of reality: Where do we shop for "moderate" cosmetics and jewelry? The same counters are filled with unending displays of more, more, and more.

People may think they will be satisfied with "just a little," but let's look at some insight from Vani Marshall, a former Hindu, who comes from a lineage of Hindu Brahmin priests:

"It's written in Song of Solomon 2:15, 'Take us the foxes, the little foxes, that spoil the vines: for our vines have tender grapes.' Foxes sometime in search of food enter into the grape orchards where they devour the grapes and spoil the farmer's crop. Little foxes, however, are too small to reach the grape bunches so they chew on vines that damage and kill the whole plant. Instead of the farmer losing just his crop, little foxes cause him to lose his vine which is disastrous.

"Some things Christians do or allow that they might think are little or insignificant can also be disastrous. Many young people are embracing a dangerous 'little fox' or seemingly 'little thing' that may seem harmless to them. In order to be 'trendy,' many are showing off ear, nose, tongue, eyebrow, and navel jewels and rings attached to their pierced flesh. Some even have these piercings done on unspeakable parts of their bodies. These are abnormal and unnatural.

"Many are not aware of the spiritual dangers in such practices, and I don't mean to condemn any who may have already had piercings on their bodies. However, I urge you to seek the Lord as to further involvement in this practice. The Lord loves everyone, no matter what we are currently doing. His desire, however, is to show us a better way.

"Many young people are getting body piercings and tattoos in rebellion against their parents' advice. Men make statements of their rebellion by wearing earrings designed to show they are either 'macho' or homosexual. When youth despise and rebel against their parents, it is very displeasing to the Lord. One of the Ten Commandments is a mandate to honor our parents (Exodus 20:12). Colossians 3:20 states 'Children, obey your parents in all things: for this is well pleasing unto the Lord.'

"Some people argue for jewelry saying that most of the women in our society wear earrings. Some use this as an excuse for the bizarre body piercings they are flaunting. The Lord always judges what we do by our motives. He looks on our hearts.

"The Word of God in Isaiah 3:16-24 speaks of a generation of women that will be alive at the coming of the Lord who will be judged severely for their flirting and their haughtiness. We are living in the days written about in II Timothy 3:1-7: Please read this passage.

"If you have been one that has been led away by lust or have been rebellious against your parents, you can come to the Lord and repent and He will give you a new start and a desire to live a holy and obedient life unto God."

– Vani Marshall

We each arrive at moments in our lives when
we must ask ourselves,
"Am I following God's will, or mine?
Am I living His will on earth as it is in heaven"
(Matthew 6:10)?

"I desire to do your will, O my God;
your law is within my heart"
(Psalm 40:8, NIV).

I'm happy! I hope you're happy! If you're not, ask God to speak into your life. Happy is the person God corrects (Job 5:17). Check out these words of Jesus: **"If ye know these things, happy are ye if ye do them" (John 13:17).**

Grace doesn't give us permission to lead selfish, pleasure-seeking lives. Grace supplies the power God's people need to live in the Spirit. (See Romans 6:1.)

As I thought about the grace of God and how we are reflections of that grace, I noticed the prism hanging in my kitchen window. It is just a piece of glass. There is really nothing special about it—that is, until the light shines through it!

When light hits a prism, it gives off beautiful reflections that change as the light hits it at different angles. Though the light is the same, the reflection can change. It doesn't look as if it has much inside but it gives off an array of color and brilliance. The maker knew exactly how to create the perfect cuts so the prism could be radiant.

It is amazing what light can do with something that at first glance seems ordinary. Think about this: We were created to reflect the goodness of God! How do we reflect the Light? The Creator molded us perfectly to reflect an image of beauty, purity, and holiness.

"For the grace of God (His unmerited favor and blessing) has come forward (appeared) for the deliverance from sin and the eternal salvation for all mankind. It has trained us to reject and renounce all ungodliness (irreligion) and worldly (passionate) desires, to live discreet (temperate, self-controlled), upright, devout (spiritually whole) lives in this present world" (Titus 2:11-12, AMP).

We have freedom from sin, but not freedom to sin. The truth is, my friend, God purposely placed some "shalt nots" in the Bible. Some things will always be "thou shalt nots" for our own good. And God said, "Beloved, follow not that which is evil, but that which is good" (III John 11).

If the Lord is prompting you to change, please don't override His voice. Won't you open your heart and make it a matter of prayer? The truth is most people don't *want* to sacrifice. I don't roll out of bed, have a morning stretch, and say, "What do I like that I can give up today?"

Some attempt to justify compromise in areas of biblical lifestyle teachings—God's call to holiness and righteousness—while yelling loudly, "Legalism! Legalism!"

Holiness is both inward and outward and includes attitudes, actions, and appearance along with physical and spiritual stewardship. Is it honest to say holiness has nothing to do with the outer person? We know we aren't to use our bodies for sin. We live in a physical world. What we do with our bodies affects our relationships with others, including God! Since we are all in the process of perfecting holiness (II Corinthians 7:1) we must be careful to extend grace to one another (Colossians 3:12-13).

Regardless of our own positions of the consecration issues we have discussed in *The Pure Path Series*, we need to pray and study and study and pray. We need to know if Christian standards are unsupported church rules or if they are based on the Word of God. It's important to know that our faith and doctrine are based on sound biblical principles.

When it comes right down to the bottom line, I really don't want my beauty based on something that can be removed with a wet

Kleenex or unfastened by a metal clasp. But never fear, my friend! God has an everlasting supply of Holy Ghost beautifier!

The verses of Scripture in this study are not just empty words but are firmly established since the beginning of time. The psalmist David knew this and wrote the following immortal words: "For ever, O LORD, thy word is settled in heaven. Thy faithfulness is unto all generations: thou hast established the earth, and it abideth" (Psalm 119:89-90). Just as surely as the world still stands, God's Word still stands. We have heard from the prophets of the Old Testament. We have witnessed through the Word of God the historical accounts of Jacob and others. Both Peter and Paul have affirmed it, as well. We've heard real-life personal testimonies and looked at present-day examples. The question remains: What saith thou?

And as you consider that all-important question, I ask you to please consider the following verses of Scripture:

"Whatsoever we ask, we receive of him, because we keep his commandments, and do those things that are pleasing in his sight" (I John 3:22).

"Find out what pleases the Lord" (Ephesians 5:10, NIV).

"If ye continue in my word, then are ye my disciples indeed" (John 8:31).

"Let no one deceive you with empty words, for because of such things God's wrath comes on those who are disobedient. Therefore do not be partners with them" (Ephesians 5:6-7, NIV).

Following is the testimony of a young Christian girl who wishes to remain anonymous:

- -

"After the Lord touched my heart, I was told by a friend that body piercing and tattoos were wrong. I was immediately defensive and confused. I wanted to follow the Lord and do what was right in His eyes.

"We couldn't find anything that directly said you should not pierce your body but I decided to pray about whether it was right for me to have a body piercing and tattoo. During the time I was praying and seeking God about this, He led me to verses of Scripture such as I Corinthians 6:19: 'Do you not know that your body is a temple of the Holy Spirit, who is in you, whom you have received from God? You are not your own; you were bought at a price. Therefore honor God with your body' (NIV). I was also convicted by I Corinthians 3:16: 'Don't you know that you yourselves are God's temple and that God's Spirit lives in you? If anyone destroys God's temple, God will destroy him; for God's temple is sacred, and you are that temple' (NIV).

"I felt that I had harmed my body by tattooing it and piercing it. I passed out when I got my body pierced and came close to passing out when I got my tattoo. I went through a lot of pain to look cool. I felt it was wrong for me to have pierced and tattooed my body, especially because the reasons behind both were vanity and pride. Between vanity and pride and harming the body that the Lord had created, I knew that I had sinned.

"Now I can see that I was not honoring God with my body by piercing it and putting a permanent mark on it. Although I was able to remove my piercing, my tattoo is not something that I can just wash away. It is on my leg to stay.

"I know the Lord has forgiven me. His grace and love are so amazing. I was living a sinful, ungodly life and then I found the Lord. Jesus died for us all, and God raised Him from the dead so that our sins can be forgiven and that we may be cleansed of our iniquities. Now, we can enter into an amazing love relationship with Him.

"The point of this testimony is to share how I was convicted of sin in my life. It doesn't matter what the sin was. We all need to repent and follow the Lord. If we love Him, we will obey Him."

– Anonymous

Consider the following words spoken by Jesus: "If ye love me, keep my commandments" (John 14:15). He went on to say, "If a man love me, he will keep my words: and my Father will love him, and we will come unto him, and make our abode with him" (John 14:23).

John wrote, "This is love for God: to obey his commands. And his commands are not burdensome, for everyone born of God overcomes the world" (I John 5:3-4, NIV).

The psalmist wrote, "Thy testimonies are very sure: holiness becometh thine house, O LORD, forever!" (Psalm 93:5). God no longer lives in buildings. *We* are His building! He lives in us—Bible-believing Christians—and therefore holiness should "become" us. It is something that should be there for the rest of our lives!

"Hereby we do know that we know him, if we keep his commandments. He that saith, I know him, and keepeth not his commandments, is a liar, and the truth is not in him. But whoso keepeth his word, in him verily is the love of God perfected: hereby know we that we are in him" (I John 2:3-5). These are absolutes from which we must never allow ourselves to walk away.

151

Endnotes

1 "Only Two Percent of Women Describe Themselves as Beautiful; New Global Study Uncovers Desire for Broader Definition of Beauty," September 29, 2004. *www.campaignforrealbeauty.com/press.asp?section=news&id=110*

2 *http://dictionary.reference.com/browse/beauty*

3 Ibid.

4 Ted Polhemus. *Hot Bodies, Cool Styles: New Techniques in Self Adornment* (London: Thames & Hudson, Ltd., 2004).

5 Mike Parker Pearson. *The Archaeology of Death & Burial* (College Station, TX, Texas A&M University, 2002).

6 *http://www.vanishingtattoo.com/images/contest2/stiched_5.Pazyryk_300.jpg*

7 John A. Rush. *Spiritual Tattoo, a Culture of Tattooing, Piercing, Scarification, Branding and Implants* (Berkley, CA: Frog, Ltd., 2005).

8 Michael D. Coe. *The Maya* (New York: Frederick A. Praeger, 1967).

9 Rush. *Spiritual Tattoo.*

10 "Becoming Someone Else: Genocide and Kidnapped Armenian Women." *http://www.genocide-museum.am/eng/online_exhibition_2.php*

11 Steve Gilbert. *The Tattoo History Source Book* (New York, NY: Juno Books, 2000).

12 James Freeman. *The New Manners and Customs of the Bible* (Gainesville, FL: Bridge-Logos Publishers, 1998).

13 Charles Erdman. *The Book of Leviticus* (Ada, MI: Baker Publishing Group, 1982).

14 *http://judaism.about.com/od/conversi2/f/tatoos_burial.htm*

15 Ibid.

16 Polhemus. *Hot Bodies, Cool Styles.*

17 *http://www.sterneck.net/ritual/fakir-musafar-modern-primitives/index.php*

18 Ibid.

19 Ibid.

20 Ibid.

21 Ibid.

22 Ibid.

23 Polhemus. *Hot Bodies, Cool Styles*.

24 Rush. *Spiritual Tattoo*.

25 Ibid.

26 *http://www.meganfoxdaily.com/info/tattoos.php*

27 *http://todayentertainment.today.msnbc.msn.com/_news/2012/02/28/10529160-megan-fox-details-the-pain-of-having-her-tattoos-removed?lite*

28 Rush. *Spiritual Tattoo*.

29 Ibid.

30 Ibid.

31 Bonnie Graves. *Tattooing and Body Piercing (Perspective on Physical Health)* (Mankato, MN: Capstone Press, 2000).

32 *http://www.moderneprimitives.com/*

33 R. W. B. Scutt and Christopher Gotch. *Art, Sex and Symbol: The Mystery of Tattooing* (New York, NY: Cornwall Books, 1974).

34 Ibid.

35 Timothy A. Roberts, M.D. and Sheryl A. Ryan, M.D. *Tattooing and High-Risk Behavior in Adolescents, Division of Adolescent Medicine* (Rochester, NY: Strong Children's Research Center, University of Rochester School of Medicine, 2001).

36 Ibid.

37 *http://www.childresearch.net/resource/news/2002/200207.htm#2*

38 Rush. *Spiritual Tattoo*.

[39] J. Anderson Black. *The Story of Jewelry* (New York, NY: William Morrow & Company, Inc., 1974).

[40] Graves. *Tattooing and Body Piercing*.

[41] Black. *The Story of Jewelry*.

[42] Wilhelm Gesenius and Samuel Prideaux Tregelles. *Gesenius' Hebrew and Chaldee Lexicon to the Old Testament Scriptures: Translated, with Additions, and Corrections from the Author's Thesaurus and Other Works* (London: Samuel Bagster & Sons, Limited, 1857).

[43] *http://bible.cc/luke/15-22.htm*

[44] *http://dictionary.reference.com*

[45] Ibid.

[46] *http://www.blueletterbible.org*

[47] Maggie Angeloglou. *A History of Make-up* (West Sussex, UK: Littlehampton Book Services Ltd., 1970).

[48] Ibid.

[49] Ibid.

[50] Ibid.

[51] Ibid.

[52] Subhamoy Das. "Bindi: The Great Indian Forehead Art." *http://hinduism.about.com/od/bindis/a/bindi.htm*

[53] Angeloglou. *A History of Make-up*.

[54] Richard Morris. *Old English Homilies and Homiletic Treatises of the Twelfth and Thirteenth Centuries* (London: N. Trubner & Company, 1868).

[55] Ibid.

[56] Ibid.

[57] Angeloglou. *A History of Make-up*.

[58] Ibid.

[59] Ibid.

[60] Ibid.

61 Ibid.

62 Ibid.

63 Ibid.

64 Ibid.

65 Ibid.

66 Ibid.

67 "Pots of Promise." *http://www.economist.com/node/1795852*

68 Angeloglou. *A History of Make-up.*

69 *Holy Bible.* Young's Literal Translation.

70 *Holy Bible.* New Living Translation.

71 *http://bible.cc/hosea/2-2.htm*

72 Ibid.

73 *Holy Bible.* The Message.

74 Augustin Calmet and Charles Taylor. *Calmet's Dictionary of the Holy Bible: With the Biblical Fragments, Volume 1, Fifth Edition* (London: Holdsworth and Ball, 1830).

75 Ibid.

76 *http://www.ccel.org/ccel/smith_w/bibledict.html*

77 Calmet and Taylor. *Calmet's Dictionary of the Holy Bible.*

78 *http://www.ccel.org/ccel/smith_w/bibledict.html*

79 Ibid.

80 *http://dictionary.reference.com*

81 Herbert S. Zim. *Our Wonderful World, Vol. No. 5* (New York, NY: Grolier, Inc., 1966).

82 "Pots of Promise." *http://www.economist.com/node/1795852*

83 C. S. Lewis. *Mere Christianity* (New York, NY: HarperCollins, 1980).

Books Available from
More to Life

- -

The Girl in the Dress: Uncovering the Mystery of Modesty—In an easy-to-read style, practical insights and scriptural references explore biblical modesty. As we live and dress according to the Word of God, our inner beauty will take over, and the outward result will be one that makes us truly beautiful. For all ages.

Covered by Love: The Uncut Mystery—It's So Much More Than Hair—In a clear, thorough manner, this book lays out the positive message of obedience, purpose, and blessing concerning women's hair. Read it with your boys so they will gain an appreciation for the godly women who embrace these principles. For all ages.

Alive in Him: Learning to Live Abundantly in Christ—A study for all ages that walks one through repentance, the new birth, and how to live for God. Wonderful for new converts, Sunday school use, and Bible study groups. Ideal for prison ministry.

More to Life Bible Study Series
- *Finding God's Favor*
- *Pursuing God's Plan*
- *Walking God's Way*

This series is a proven, effective tool for reaching friends, family, coworkers, and others with a greater understanding of God's plan of salvation. Excellent for small group studies. Four lessons per book. Also available in Spanish.

Parents and Daughters Talk: Helping Your Daughter Make Right Choices—This book will help open dialogue with your daughter about moral purity. We must provide our daughters with not only technical/medical information, but also help her in making the right choices for her whole person, her whole life.

Parents and Sons Talk: Helping Your Son Make Right Choices—This book will help open dialogue with your son about moral purity choices facing young men growing up in an increasingly promiscuous world. Remember, if parents don't talk to their sons, somebody will.

Praying the Word Effectively—Promises for all occasions in life are found throughout Scripture. This selection of verses will awaken your desire to search for more of God's promises. Learn to pray the Word and be effective in your prayers for all of life's situations.

The Good Life — Success is measured in many ways, and today's young women want it all. This study defines success through the Word of God. An excellent witnessing tool. Great for personal study for pre-teen and teen girls.

These books are available through Ladies Ministries.
Call 314-837-7304 ext. 412 or email *ladies@upci.org*.
Discount prices also available.

To be assured of Bible-based literature,
always look for these registered trademarks.

THROUGH GOD'S WORD